DANISH BALLADS

DANISH BALLADS

TRANSLATED BY

E. M. SMITH-DAMPIER

CAMBRIDGE
AT THE UNIVERSITY PRESS
1920

CAMBRIDGE UNIVERSITY PRESS
Cambridge, New York, Melbourne, Madrid, Cape Town,
Singapore, São Paulo, Delhi, Mexico City

Cambridge University Press
The Edinburgh Building, Cambridge CB2 8RU, UK

Published in the United States of America by Cambridge University Press, New York

www.cambridge.org
Information on this title: www.cambridge.org/9781107691544

First published 1920
First paperback edition 2013

A catalogue record for this publication is available from the British Library

ISBN 978-1-107-69154-4 Paperback

PREFACE

So far as possible, I have reproduced the metrical variations of the original Ballads, and striven in general rather for literal accuracy than poetical effect.

All proper names are to be pronounced after the Danish fashion—with the one exception of "Sir Klaus Krummerdike" ("Niels Ebbeson," Revised Conclusion, v. 46)—a lapse which, from a sorely-tried rhymester's point of view, surely deserves rather mercy than judgment.

The Burdens should, of course, be repeated with each verse, but, for convenience' sake, I have followed the modern custom in placing them only at beginning and end of the Ballads.

I am deeply indebted to the late Dr. Axel Olrik, who gave me invaluable criticism on my work as a translator. His Introduction to *Danske Folkeviser i Udvalg* (Copenhagen) is indispensable to the student. To his literary executors, Hr. Hans Ellekilde and Frøken I. Falbe Hansson, I am indebted for leave to make use of some of his ballad-versions.

My thanks are due also to Messrs. Andrew Melrose, Ltd., by whose courtesy I am enabled to reprint many translations previously published.

E. M. SMITH-DAMPIER.

London, 1920.

CONTENTS

CONTENTS

MISCELLANEOUS BALLADS

DANISH BALLADS

INTRODUCTION

It may be assumed that the student who ap-
proaches the Danish Ballads has already acquired
some acquaintance with the prevailing theories as
to the origin of Ballads in general. On that dark
and debatable question I am unqualified to enter.
To the earnest beginner I commend Dr. T. F.
Henderson's excellent Cambridge Manual *The
Ballad in Literature*, where the opinions of
Child, Gummere, Kittredge, and other authorities, are discussed with lucidity, learning, and
common-sense. Suffice it here and now to say
that those who push to extremes the theory of
Communal Authorship must be capable of belief
in that mythological personage who was born of
nine mothers. While some Ballads (with their
Incremental Repetition and so forth) were obviously created between leader and chorus in the
Dance, others, no less obviously, were the work of
individual poets. As the nineteenth century had
its Walter Scott and its Hawker of Moorwinstow,

B

so earlier ages had the anonymous minstrels who stamped the mark of original genius on "Niels Ebbeson" and "Sir Patrick Spens."

" At the period when these songs were born, classes were mingled together, or rather did not as yet exist. The people was one ; it was the *élite*, the best among them, who interpreted what all felt, but all could not express—who sang in the name of all. And thus it is that this poetry belongs to the populace as a whole. . . . It resembles a stone constantly rolled by the waves " (Pineau).

Child, moreover, points out that the British Ballad "was not originally the property of the common orders among the people" — and in Denmark, says Henderson, "it was fostered and favoured more particularly by the upper classes, and was for some centuries the chief medium of literary expression and culture."

In Denmark, as elsewhere, the more primitive forms of the Ballad were closely connected with the Dance—the *carole*, or circular dance with joined hands, accompanied by the voice ; a pastime which still survives in the Faroë Islands. The word *Ballad*, indeed, is derived from the South Italian *ballare* = to dance, which in its turn comes from the Greek. The Teutonic tribes, whose sword-dances are mentioned by Tacitus, may, in the beginning, have learnt dancing from the Celts. Be that as it may, the round dance became popular throughout Europe during the early Middle Ages (roughly speaking, between 1149–1400), and took the North by storm, from the King's court to the Icelandic farmstead. The dance-songs made light of frontiers, just as the Australian corroborees pass, irrespective of language, from tribe to tribe. Vainly did Saxo Grammaticus record his opinion that "such mountebank antics" (gøglerspring) were unworthy of persons of quality. Every knight had his own dancing-ground—as do Papuan chiefs at the present day. Vainly did the Church frown on a pastime associated with Beltane fires, and other unhallowed survivals of paganism. Absalon, it is true, when in 1158 he became Bishop of Sjælland, put a stop to light-heeled frolic among the merry monks of Eskilø. The Copenhagen clergy in 1425 forbade "heathen" songs and dances on the Feast of S. John. But the churchyard was still the popular place to dance in, especially on the wake-nights of the greater festivals, when the people assembled from far and near. England behaved no better; a shocking record exists of an English priest, so obsessed by the refrain which had rung in his ears all night, that he began the Mass with "myn hertë swete!"

The leader of the Dance sang the Ballad proper: the other dancers came in as chorus with the Burden or Refrain. Some Burdens merely imitate

instrumental music ; such are our own Hey nonny
nonny, Tirly low (the shepherd's pipe)—the
Danish Hejt lejt lejtli, tra fal de ral, etc. Others
were derived from the Ballad itself, which was
originally a lyrical outburst improvised by the
singer.

Here is a gay example from the Icelandic :

> " Fair the swan is singing
> All the summer-tide :
> Sweet it is to dance and play
> My lily white !
>   Fair the swan is singing " (Burde n).

Or, in graver mood :

> " Heavy are my sorrows,
>   A load of lead to bear,
> Burnt are all the castles
>   Were builded new and fair.''

(This was sung by the Icelander Thord Andresson
when treacherously captured by Gissur the Earl,
1264.)

A list of Icelandic Dance-Burdens is given in
the *Corpus Poeticum Boreale*.

The beginning of the thirteenth century in-
augurated a new fashion. Narrative poetry—
originally a separate art—was combined with the
dance-lyric. Fables, for instance, were borrowed
from the Troubadours, the Minnesingers, and the
various foreign minstrels attached to the Danish

court. The lyrics were sometimes retained as introductory stanzas, sometimes broken up into Burdens. Thus the song :

> " The King he rules the castle
> And over all the land,
> And over many a warrior bold
> With shining sword in hand,"

lent its first line as Burden to a Ballad of King Didrik :

> " King Didrik sits in Brattingsborg,
> And far and wide looks he :
> Oh, none know I in all the world
> Who may my equal be !
> The King he rules the castle."

Every Ballad, in time, came to have its own introductory stanza, calculated to arouse the hearer's attention and attune it to the story which followed—had also its own Burden, which echoed the principal theme. But many have survived shorn of both adjuncts : and a few have borrowed Burdens, sometimes far from appropriate.

The Danish Ballads, like all others, deal with love, warfare, and witchcraft. Like all others, they are pagan at heart. Some of their themes are peculiar to Denmark, some common to all Europe. The similarity, for instance, between certain Danish and Scottish Ballads suggests that the one country borrowed them directly from the other. The editors of the *C.P.B.* (where a list may be found) give the lead in the matter to Scotland ; but other authorities are of a different opinion. Generally speaking, it is acknowledged that Denmark's literary output was influenced far less by Britain than by France and the other Latin countries.

But, be the themes what they may, the Danish Ballads inform them with their own characteristic spirit—the glamour and grimness of the North. The battle-scenes show us glimpses of Bersark fury, and weapons with demon souls. The Dark Powers in the Ballads of magic are those born of long winter nights and misty waters. Here and there we meet with the gods of Valhalla, and the heroes sung in Old Norse Lays. Woman, in the love-ballads, is no Troubadour's divinity, but a human helpmeet of warriors—brave, shrewd, strong-minded, occasionally strong-armed to boot. As for humour, while we have rollicking man-at-arms fun of the "Kinmont Willie" type, and some dry, pawky, Scots-like wit, a few Ballads charm us with such a delicate, wistful archness as flowers again in Andersen's fairy-tales. There are, indeed, a number of Satirical Ballads, whose characters—gaffer and gammer, wandering fiddler, Bishop's Daughter, and Mighty Maid—burlesque the heroes and heroines of the Ballads of chivalry.

These, however, from the poetical standpoint, are of little or no significance.

The social conditions depicted in these Ballads are, in many respects, peculiar to Scandinavia. The atmosphere is distinctly democratic. Denmark had no school of court-poetry, no minstrel-class corresponding to the Troubadours and Minnesingers. Her kings made foreign marriages, and imported foreign talent; no petty courts, princely or ducal, existed to serve as centres of culture.[1] The native singers found patrons among the native gentry, or lesser nobility—the Knights, whose position in many respects was that of the old-time English country squire. With the tastes, interests, and outlook of this class the Ballads as a whole are chiefly concerned.

Apart from such ballad-cycles as those dealing with the two Valdemars, the King mostly appears merely as a power in the background—a *deus* (or, more frequently, a *diabolus*) *ex machinâ*. Of devoted loyalty, of patriotism identified with the royal person, we find traces only in the most ancient historical Ballads—with an occasional after-echo such as the Page's words in the "King-Slaying in Finderup" (No. 6). His courtiers and

---

[1] With one exception—the ducal court at Gottorp in Sleswik; but its intellectual influence suffered from the constant warfare among the Holstein nobility.

"captains" are derided by the country-bred minstrel : "So long have they served in the royal court they can bear nor heat nor smoke!"

The Church, too, is only seen afar off—affects the Knight chiefly through the convent school, where young ladies are educated. The Burgher is an unknown quantity. Only in a late (fifteenth-century) Ballad do we hear of the rich merchants, with houses in "Randers street," whose gilded vanes gleam over the walls, shaming the castles of envious Knights.

The Yeoman (Bonde) class was that with which this lesser nobility was most intimately connected —the class whence it sprang, wherein it was merged after the Peasant Revolt of 1584. Well-born youths are described as "noble yeomen's sons" (ædelige Bøndersønner), and a yeoman's wife makes occasional appearance as heroine of a Ballad. The Knight defends the yeoman against pillage and oppression. The two classes, however, are distinct, and keep their distance. The Knight may farm his own land—may even be found holding the plough—but he is, none the less, the yeoman's social superior. His daughter, if she weds a yeoman, must "doff the scarlet fine, and don the wadmal grey."

The Knight was served by his Squires (svende) —sometimes of yeoman extraction, but more

frequently landless nobles, or younger sons — his
lady by her Maidens. The former received
wages, and a training in chivalry ; the latter learnt
polite deportment, household duties, and needle-
craft. Thus in our own " Fause Foodrage " :

> " And ye sall teach my gay goss-hawk
>   To wield baith bow and brand,
>   And I sall teach your turtle-doo
>   To lay gowd wi' her hand."

The Knight's existence, then, much resembled
the Viking's—was passed in warfare, with intervals
of agriculture, of sport, or even of commerce.
That it was lived chiefly " on the land " is shown
by a thousand touches and images racy of the soil.
The arrows stick "thick as hay" in Knight Stig's
mantle ; young Engelbret hews down his foes
" as the peasant cuts down corn." The Knight's
absences from home are frequently mentioned—
absences on foray, on trading journeys, or at the
Thing—the Yeomen's Thing or District Council,
distinct from the great national Land's Thing.
There the local notabilities met to settle local
affairs, conclude bargains, and dispose of their
children's hands in marriage (see " Lovel and
John," No. 28).

As this Knight was to some extent a country
squire, so his dwelling rather resembled a fortified
farm than a feudal castle. Its garth (gaard),

surrounded by a palisade, contained a collection of separate buildings, mostly built of wood, and thatched with straw or reed. The linden tree which shaded the garth, and the castle gate which afforded a glimpse of the outer world, figure largely in the Ballads.

The main building contained the principal living-rooms, and was adorned with carved beams projecting from the gables—which beams, in process of time, were replaced by weather-vanes. Access both to ground-floor and upper storey (højeloft) was obtained by means of an outside gallery-staircase (svalegang, højloftssvale), where the traveller was wont to hang up his cloak (axlèr sit Skind) ere he entered the hall.

Refuge from attack was to be found in another building, the Stone-hall (stenstue)—or, where this was lacking, in the nearest church tower. (The term " stenstue " is occasionally applied to the main building, should it happen to be built of stone, but this is exceptional.)

> " A house have I walled round with stone
>   That stands my garth within ;
> I wot when I take refuge there
>   I fear not a hundred men ! "

Another most important building was the Maiden's Bower, richly adorned, and " locked right well " lest it be " broken " by over-importu-

nate suitors. Those fathers were censured as
"inexperienced" who built it in too remote a
spot.

A few Ballads speak of castles with dungeons
and fortified gates, but these were few and far
between.

Towards the close of the Middle Ages manners
underwent a change; antique simplicity was
corrupted. These unpretentious knights were
swamped by the rise of a more powerful nobility,
who united their estates through intermarriages,
and followed the fashions of the court. The
round dance was driven from the castle to the
farmhouse. Persons of quality, however, retained
a certain amount of interest in the old Ballads;
and to this interest the fact is owing that Ballads
in Denmark were earlier written down than those
of any other European country. The young
lady of the sixteenth century was wont to keep
an album, wherein verses were inscribed by her
friends; and, amid love-complaints, compliments,
moral emblems, and so forth, the old national
folk-poems found their place. From these
albums were gathered the first collections of
Ballads. Every lady's bower had its own collection—and the singing of the Ballads during the
long winter evenings led to much disastrous
dilution of the original texts.

With the coming in of the seventeenth-century Pastoral, the fashionable career of the Ballad was over, but its value was recognized from the literary and historical point of view ; and the business of collection began in earnest. Royal patronage was not lacking. In June 1586 Queen Sophie visited Tycho Brahé in his observatory on the isle of Hveen, was storm-bound for three days, and entertained with Ballads by another guest, Anders Vedel the historian. He promised her a collection, which promise materialized in the shape of *Queen Sophie's Ballad Book*, followed shortly by another based on the great folio MS. of the Odensee nunnery (Karen Brahé's library).

The yeoman and peasant, meanwhile, remained faithful to the Ballad as a means of recreation, and continued to import new ones, mostly from Germany. Ballads were sung in Jutland until late in the nineteenth century, and many of these, not previously written down, were collected during the national revival of the eighteen-forties.

Danish Ballads were not only collected in MS., but printed and published earlier than those elsewhere — Vedel's *A Hundred Choice Danish Ballads* in 1591 ; *Tragica, or Love Ballads* in 1657. Peter Syr's enlarged collection followed in 1695. *Danish Ballads from the Middle Ages* was published in 1811–12 by Abrahamson, Nyerip, and Rahbek ;

and then came Sven Grundtvig's epoch-making *Denmark's Ancient Ballads* (1853), which contains every known version of every specimen, with critical and historical prefaces.

An excellent popular selection, by Axel Olrik and Ida Falbe Hansen (*Danske Folkeviser i Udvalg*), was published in 1912 ; and from the ballad-versions given therein I have prepared the translations which follow.

HISTORICAL BALLADS

I, II

VALDEMAR AND TOVE (A) AND (B)

THE historical foundation for these two Ballads
amounts only to this ; that Valdemar I, or the
Great (1157–82), had a mistress named Tove ;
that she bore him a son, Christopher ; and that
the King found it expedient to put her away, and
ally himself with his opponent Knud Magnusson
by marrying his half-sister Sophia. Nothing is
known of Tove's fate ; her death at her rival's
hands is a figment of the popular fancy.

The older (A) version (preserved in Iceland) is
chiefly interesting from its picture of Tove in
the character of that perfect lover so dear to the
mediæval masculine mind — the Patient Grizel,
the Burd Ellen, who knows no jealousy where
her lord's affections are concerned. Valdemar's
apparently tactless questions are designed to bring
out the contrast between the meek submission of
the mistress and the frank hatred of the wife.

The Danish or B version, probably composed

some fifty years later, takes a more human point of view. It sacrifices historical accuracy to dramatic effect by handing over Sophia's son Knud (afterwards King) to Tove.

I

VALDEMAR AND TOVE, 1157   (A)

1

King Valdemar sailed here and there,
  —Good sooth,—
He wed little Soffi, a maid so fair,
  —King Valdemar he wooed them both.

2

"Harken, Tove mine, and hear,
Dost thou hold Queen Soffi dear?"

3

"Less dear to me, I ween
Than my son, I hold the Queen.

4

"I will give her a good grey steed,
And the name of Queen she shall bear indeed."

5

"Harken, Soffi mine, and hear,
Dost thou hold my Tove dear?"

6

"I love her all so well
As the wild wolf in the dell.

7

"I will give her castles three,
She may burn therein for me!"

8

The Queen she spake to her page so small:
"Now bring Tovelille in to the hall!"

9

So fain was Tove to see the Queen
She clad her at night by the taper's sheen.

10

She clad her in a kirtle of blue,
At every seam red gold shone through.

11

She clad her in a silken sark,
Of eleven maidens the handiwork.

12

She wrapped her in a cloak of red,
And thus to see the Queen she sped.

13

"Art fainer with the King to speak
Or the bath with me to seek?"

14

"Far fainer with the King I'd speak
Than the bath with thee I'd seek!"

15

Soffi the Queen was strong of arm,
She thrust her in to work her harm.

16

So hot she heated the fire beneath
That Tovelille could scarce draw breath.

17

"Help me, Christopher, son of mine!
Soffi will slay me in dule and pine!"

C

18

"Oh how should I give help to thee?
Twelve armed men have hold of me!"

19

Up spake the King, his men among,
"Why goeth not Tove to Evensong?"

20

Up spake Queen Soffi, red with wrath:
"Thy Tove is wearied with her bath!"

21

"Well, Soffi, will I pay thy pain,
Shalt never sleep in my bed again!

22

" Better was she with one cow for dower
Than thou art, Soffi, with town and tower!

23

" Better was Tove in silken sark
Than thou art, Soffi, with all thy goldsmith's work!

24

" Dearer is Tovelil, tho' she be dead,
Than thou, for all thy gold so red!"

25

The way was long, the way was drear,
The King himself bore up the bier.
—Good sooth.
King Valdemar, he wooed them both.

II
VALDEMAR AND TOVE (B)

1

GAY went the dance in King Valdemar's hall,
There danced the Queen with maidens small;
—By my troth; King Valdemar he wooed them both.

2

There danced the Queen with maidens fair,
There danced Tove with waving hair.

3

"Harken now, Tove, my playfellow sweet!
Gird up thy silk skirts around thy feet."

4

"Small praise from me the King should gain
If I might not trail a silken train."

5

"Tove, my playfellow, tell to me
How did the King get his will o' thee?"

6

"The King he won his will of me,
For stronger than I the King was he.

7

"I was but a maiden small
Dwelling in my father's hall.

8

"So little and fair by the door stood I
When the King and all his merry men they came a-
    riding by.

9

"By nine, by ten, his knights he sent,
But never for their commands I went.

10

" The King he came himself with all his merry men,
And I, Tovelille, must follow then ! "

11

" Tove, my playfellow, tell thou me
What bridal-gift he gave to thee."

12

" He gave me a chest of golden sheen
Such as was never in Denmark seen.

13

" He gave to me nine rings ot gold
That Sweden's Queen did have and hold.

14

" He clad me in silk and in scarlet gay ;
Thou and all thy maidens ne'er went in such array."

15

Up spake Queen Soffi in anger wild :
" 'Twas enough, I trow, for a yeoman's child !

16

" By God the Lord, while I breathe and live,
Less by half to thee shall he give ! "

17

The Queen she wrapped her in cloak of vair,
To speak with King Valdemar did she fare.

18

" Now answer what I ask of thee ;
Why lovest thou Tove more than me ? "

19

" For this Tovelille to me is dear,
Because she hath two sons that serve my person near.

20

"When Flensborg town I first rode by
Christopher bore my banner so high.

21

"When first I rode to Holsterland
Knud bore my banner in his right hand."

22

Winters twain were gone and past
Ere the Queen got her will at last.

23

All on a holy Christmas day
Tove sought the kirk to pray.

24

Tovelille fared forth in the street,
Golden silk and samite went floating round her feet.

25

Forth from her window the Queen did spy,
She saw proud Tovelil passing by.

26

The Queen she spake to her maidens three :
"Now bid proud Tovelil come to me!"

27

Tove wrapped her in cloak of vair,
And unto Soffi's bower did fare.

28

"Lithe now and listen, proud Tove, to me ;
I will seek the bath to-night with thee."

29

"Ne'er of the bath can I have my fill ;
I'll do thy bidding with right good-will!"

30

The Queen she spake to her pages three :
"Take heed that the bath is hot for me !

31

"Heat it hot, and heat it red !
There shall Tovelil lie dead !"

32

Tovelil went in before.
The Queen herself she locked the door.

33

"Here is no water, here is no lye !
Let me out for the sake of GOD on high !"

34

Christopher went riding by,
He heard his mother wail and cry.

35

He struck the door a blow so stout
That bolt and nail came leaping out.

36

He burst the door with rage and wrath,
He bore his mother forth from the bath.

37

He bore her out where the blossoms blow,
But she was dead ere first cock-crow.
—By my troth ; King Valdemar he wooed them both.

III, IV, V
THE DAGMAR BALLADS
QUEEN BENGERD

VALDEMAR II (1202–41) has been strangely dealt with by the Ballads. They are silent alike as to the warlike exploits which won him the name of Sejr, the Victorious, and the administrative reforms commemorated in his other title of Legifer. His crusade against the heathen Esthonians—even the miraculous gift of the Dannebrog, the national standard blazoned in the armorial bearings of the conquered city Reval— left popular imagination unmoved. It seized, however, on the images of his two Queens, ascribing to the one all that was liked, to the other all that was loathed, in the King's treatment of his subjects.

Dragomir the Bohemian came to Denmark in 1205, bore the King a son, Valdemar, and died two years later, probably in childbirth. From the first she was the people's darling ; her Slav name was changed to Dagmar (Dag-mø = day-maid or light-bringer) " by reason," says a contemporary chronicler, " of her great beauty."

The Ballads of her Bridal and Death were probably composed by the next generation, and have little pretension to historical accuracy. Bishop Valdemar, for instance, was not the Queen's uncle, but the King's first cousin—son of Knud Magnusson, whose sister was Valdemar's mother. In consequence of an attempt to usurp the throne, as the German Emperor's vassal, he was thrown into prison at Søberg, where he lay for fourteen years. His release in 1205 was due to the Pope's intervention, aided, as a monkish chronicle puts it, "by the loving representations of Bishop Andreas and others "— but the people, perhaps with some reason, pictured Dagmar as the peacemaker.

A second Ballad of her bridal describes her wooing by Sir Strange as the King's proxy :

> " I saw a sail fare o'er the Sound,
> —So many a pennon of gold—
> There sailed he, Sir Strange, with Dagmar the Queen."

Little is known of Valdemar's second Queen, Berengaria, except that she too was beautiful. But, since she came of a contentious and covetous family, the popular view of her character may be accurate enough. The "binding the harbours with iron bands " means the closing of them with chains, so that tribute might be exacted from incoming vessels. The Ballad's account of her death—a relishing piece of poetical justice—has no foundation in fact.

III

QUEEN DAGMAR'S BRIDAL, 1205

1

I⊤ was the Queen of Bejerland
    That to her daughter cried:
"Great honour will they show to thee
    When thou art Denmark's bride."
—They sailed from noblest Bejerland.

2

"When thou art wed to Denmark's King
    Thou shalt have pride and praise;
Now bid the peasant pay no tax,
    And he'll love thee all his days!

3

"This first boon beg thou of thy lord,
    And beg it withouten fear,
That Bishop Valdemar go free,
    Thy mother's brother dear!"

4

They spread the cloths of samite
    To lie her feet before;
They took her, the lady Dagmar,
    And led her to the shore.

5

They hoisted up their sails of silk
    All on the golden mast,
And so they sailed to Denmark
    Or e'er two months were past.

6

Down they cast their anchors
  All in the snow-white sand ;
They took her, the lady Dagmar,
  And led her first to land.

7

They took her, the lady Dagmar,
  And led her first to land ;
It was the King of Denmark
  Stretched forth his lily hand.

8

They spread the cloths of samite
  To lie her feet before ;
They led her, the lady Dagmar,
  Up to the castle door.

9

All in the morning early,
  Long ere the dawn of day,
It was the lady Dagmar
  Her bridal-gift did pray.

10

"The first boon that I beg of thee,
  I beg withouten fear ;
Let Bishop Valdemar go free,
  My mother's brother dear !

11

"The second boon I beg of thee
  'Tis with good-will, I trow ;
Loose every captive from his irons,
  And tax not the peasant's plough !"

12

"Hush thee now, Queen Dagmar,
  Speak no such words to me !
If Bishop Valdemar comes forth
  A widow he'll make of thee !"

13

She's taken off her crown of gold
  And laid it on the board :
"Oh, what shall I do in Denmark
  Since thou wilt not hear my word ?"

14

"Now bring me in Sir Strange,
  And bring Sir Knud to me !
'Tis they shall ride to Attingborg
  And set the captives free !"

15

And when he came from dungeon forth
  He could not stand nor go :
"Here have I lain eight years and more,
  Long years, I ween, and slow !"

16

She's taken out her comb of gold,
  To comb his yellow hair :
For every lock she ordered
  Down fell a bitter tear.

17

"Harken now, Queen Dagmar,
  And weep not thus for me !
For an I live but a twelvemonth
  Sore shall my vengeance be !"

18

"Now hush thee, Bishop Valdemar,
  Let be thy chiding vain !
Art thou thrown once more into Attingborg
  Thou'lt ne'er win out again !"
—They sailed from noblest Bejerland.

IV
QUEEN DAGMAR'S DEATH

1

Queen Dagmar lay in Ribe sick,
  To Ringsted did she fare ;
All the dames of Denmark's land
  She bade them seek her there.
—In Ringsted rests Queen Dagmar.

2

"Go fetch me four, go fetch me five,
  The wisest among them all !
Go fetch little Kirsten of Rise,
  The sister of Sir Karl."

3

All so modest and so mild
  She came to the bower door ;
So fain of her was Dagmar the Queen
  That she raised her head once more.

4

"Now canst thou read and canst thou write
  To help me in my need,
Then shalt thou don the scarlet fine,
  And ride my good grey steed."

5

"Oh, can I read and can I write
    I'll do it for thee full fain,
For by my troth I tell thee
    Sharper than steel is thy pain."

6

She's taken up Saint Mary's book,
    And the sheen of the golden crown
She could not see whenas she read,
    So fast her tears ran down.

7

They led her up, they led her down,
    And still her pain was sore:
"Oh, send ye word to the King our lord
    To speak with me once more!"

8

Up he stood, the little page,
    Full fain was he to speed,
He reached his saddle down from the beam
    And mounted the milk-white steed.

9

The King stood on the tower so tall
    And looked out far and wide:
"Oh, yonder I see a little page,
    And ruefully doth he ride.

10

"Yonder I see a little foot-page,
    And mournful is his mien;
Now grant, Almighty God in heaven,
    That all be well with the Queen!"

11

In he came the little foot-page,
  Before the board stood he :
"Now wilt thou speak with the Queen again
  Thou must speak right speedilie !"

12

The King smote hard upon the board
  That all the goblets rung :
"Almighty God in heaven forbid
  That Dagmar should die so young !"

13

The King he rode by Skanderborg
  With a hundred swains and one,
But when he rode by Ribe
  Then rode he all alone.

14

Oh, woe there was in the women's bower,
  And bitter dule and harm,
For the Queen, or ever the King rode up,
  Lay dead in Kirsten's arm.

15

And when he entered in the door
  He saw the bier beside :
"Now help me, God our Father in heaven,
  My bitter grief to bide !

16

"Now pray for me, dames and damsels all,
  And see that ye pray not in vain,
So fain am I to speak a word
  With Dagmar once again !"

17

Uprose the Queen upon the bier,
  And red, red were her eyne :
"Now woe is me, my noble lord,
  That thus we meet in pine !

18

"The first boon that I beg thee now
  I beg for love of me ;
Give peace to every outlawed man,
  And set the captives free.

19

"The second boon I beg thee now
  I beg for love of thee ;
Oh, take not Bengerd for thy mate,
  So sour a shrew is she !

20

"The third boon that I beg thee now
  I beg for love so dear ;
That thou let Knud, my youngest son,
  Be King in Denmark here.

21

"Ne'er need I ha' burnt in bitter pains
  By night and else by day,
Had I ne'er on the Sabbath tired my head
  And tied my ribbons gay.

22

"Now time it is I were away,
  No longer may I bide ;
The bells of heaven are ringing for me,
  And the angels wait beside."
—In Ringsted rests Queen Dagmar.

V

QUEEN BENGERD

1

ALL in the morning, long ere day,
She for her bridal-gift did pray,
—Woe be on her then, Queen Bengerd!

2

"Now give me Samsey to have and hold,
And let every maid pay a crown of gold!"

3

To Bengerd spake the King eftsoon:
"Thou must beg another boon!

4

"So many a maid lives in poverty
She cannot do it though she die!"

5

"Dear my lord, now heed my prayer,
Let no lady scarlet wear!"

6

"Oh, can she buy it with gold and fee
She may wear it full well for me!"

7

"Dear my lord, my prayer now heed,
That no son of a churl may ride a fair steed!"

8

"Oh, can he come by it in honestie
He may ride it full well for me!"

9

"Dear my lord, now give commands
To close all the havens with iron bands!"

10

"Now where shall I so much metal win
As to close all the havens with fetters in?"

11

"Up to Ribe will we fare,
We shall find good blacksmiths there.

12

"How dare the peasant hope for more
Than hut of wood and hingeless door?

13

"What more gear should a peasant gain
Than a single cow and oxen twain?

14

"For every son that his wife shall bear
A piece of gold shall be my share.

15

"A piece of gold for every son,
For every daughter half a one!"

16

The King slept first in the dawning dim,
And good Queen Dagmar appeared to him.

17

"When thou farest abroad thy foes to find
Bengerd must not bide behind!

18

"Bides Bengerd behind a year, I say,
The babe in the cradle must rue the day!"

19

"Now busk thee and boun thee, Bengerd the Queen!
Shalt fare to the foray with me, I ween."

D

20

The first shaft shot from the foeman's bark
In Bengerd's bosom found its mark.

21

Now Bengerd in darksome mould abides,
And the peasant hath oxen and kine besides.

22

Now Bengerd lies in mirk and mould,
And every maid hath her crown of gold !
—Woe be on her then, Queen Bengerd !

VI, VII, VIII

THE KING-SLAYING IN FINDERUP
MARSK STIG AND HIS LADY
EXTRACT FROM THE LONG BALLAD
OF MARSK STIG

These Ballads have been selected from a cycle
dealing with the murder of King Erik Klipping
(1259–86), and the subsequent disturbances. All
through his reign he was at feud with his
turbulent nobles ; in 1282 they extorted his
signature to a Constitution (Denmark's Magna
Carta) safeguarding the rights of the nobility and
liberties of the people ; then, since he proved
faithless, they did him to death. The murder
took place on the night of November 22, 1286 ;
his corpse was found next morning, with fifty-six

wounds, in a barn at Finderup, whither he had retired to sleep during a hunting expedition. The assassins escaped for a time, but their identity was suspected, and the young King Erik Mœndved (1286–1319) was determined to have justice. At the Parliament of Nyborg (1287) a grand jury was impanelled to try the late King's principal adversaries ; nine, mostly of one family, were found guilty and declared outlaws, the royal marshal, Stig Andersen, among them. They took refuge among the islands, whence they harried the coasts of Denmark ; and the protection afforded them by Norway gave rise to a lengthy war.

The "King-Slaying" is the earliest of the Ballads on this subject. The innocence of the King's page Rane was loudly maintained by his friends, who asserted that he, "naked and weaponless, warded his master," but evidence was forthcoming that proved his treachery.

The Ballad next in date describes the outlaws' departure from Denmark, and Stig's resolve to build a castle at Hjælm. The third of the series tells of his ill-omened dream, and his wife's attempt to explain it away—his ride to the royal castle, the Queen's taunt that he wishes to usurp the crown, and his reply that such an ambition rather befits her paramour, Drost Ove.

The young King declares him an outlaw ; Stig
threatens to keep his foot in Denmark, and
begins the building of his castle, whose looming
battlements scare the peasantry.

The fourth Ballad, " Marsk Stig and his Lady "
(No. 7), was written after a lapse of time when
the political motive for the Slaying had been
forgotten, and replaced by one more romantic,
based on a vague tradition. The King, in fact,
appears as David, and Stig as Uriah the Hittite.
The Ballad has therefore no claim to historical
accuracy ; moreover, it places the action throughout in Sjælland.

Latest of all comes "The Long Ballad of
Marsk Stig," which—after the fashion of the
"Lytell Geste of Robin Hood "—unites all the
other Ballads in a consecutive narrative, repro-
ducing them mostly word for word, yet enriching
them with its own characteristic touches. The
King's villainy is heightened by his promise to
watch over Dame Ingeborg during her husband's
absence ; " she shall suffer no more wrong than
if thyself wert home." Rane, the treacherous
page, appears as sister's son to the Dame, with
whom he plots the King's murder. After Stig's
defiance at the Thing, and before the Slaying, the
Long Ballad inserts an episode peculiar to itself ;
the amorous King goes a-hunting with Rane,

gets lost in the wood, and encounters an Elf-Maid, who, in riddling words, prophesies his imminent death.

This poem, fine as it is, foreshadows the decline of the Ballad pure and simple, and its supersession by the more lengthy and complicated Romance, or novel in verse.

There are other Ballads (not contemporary) dealing with the minor characters in the drama, which give picturesque glimpses of the outlaw's adventurous life:

> " Marstig he had daughters twain,
>   And all their lot was sorrow and pain.
>   The elder took the younger by the hand,
>   And thro' the wide world did lead her."

(Since, in some versions, the wandering maidens are the King of England's daughters, it is probable that Marsk Stig's name crept in from a semi-historical Ballad of Erik Mœndved's Bridal, wherein the young Queen begs the release of Stig's daughters from prison.)

Another sings the " Wooing of Ranild Jonson," who by threats forces his beloved from her reluctant parents:

> "Nought for their bridal bower they found
>   But the wood and the wild and the low green ground,

For sorely was he severed from friends and kinsmen.

.   .   .   .   .   .

Forests have ears, and fields have eyes ;
We must wander, my maid, as the wild swan flies,
Since we are severed both from friends and kinsmen."

VI

THE KING-SLAYING IN FINDERUP, 1285

1

So many dwell in Denmark
  Would all be masters there !
They've ridden up to Ribe
  And close disguise they wear.
—And therefore the land lies in peril.

2

They've clothed them in a close disguise
  As friars of orders grey,
And up the land they've ridden
  Their leal lord to betray.

3

They watched him in, they watched him out,
  They watched thro' time and tide,
They watched him till the woful hour
  He should to Finderup ride.

4

They rode into the goodman's garth,
  And shining spears they bore ;
Was never a man might know them
  For the monkish cowls they wore.

5

Oh, they rode in where the wax-light stood
   A-burning in the bower ;
They led him out, the youthful King,
   And that was an evil hour.

6

"Harken, Ranild Jonson,
   Wilt thou defend my life,
Half my kingdom I'll give thee,
   And my sister to thy wife !"

7

It was Ranild Jonson
   That hewed at beam and board ;
Good sooth, most like a traitor
   Did he defend his lord !

8

Oh, they've struck in at the shoulder,
   And out at the heart they smite :
"There shall be woe in all Denmark
   For the deed we ha' done this night !"

9

It was the little foot-page
   That mote not bear the sight ;
The saddle he took from the good grey steed
   And set it upon the white.

10

The saddle he took from the good grey steed
   And set it upon the white,
And he has ridden to Skanderborg
   Before the fall of night.

11

The Queen sits on the tower so tall,
   And looks forth far and wide :
" Yonder I see a little foot-page,
   And swiftly doth he ride.

12

" All on his master's steed he rides,
   And woe is me for fear !
Now watch, Almighty God in heaven,
   Over my lord so dear ! "

13

" Now GOD have mercy on his soul !
   For slain our lord doth lie ;
The King lies killed in Finderup,
   And the land is in jeopardy !

14

" Now watch ye well your castle,
   Now watch ye well your realm,
Now watch ye well your own young son
   Shall stand at Denmark's helm ! "

15

" So long as thou and I shall live,
   Though ill thy tidings be,
Fire and food in the royal court
   This shalt thou have in fee ! "
—And therefore the land lies in peril.

VII

MARSK STIG AND HIS LADY

I

IT is young Sir Marstig must journey far and wide ;
It is young King Erik that hath betrayed his bride.
—The lady she sits in Sælland, and weeps right woefully.

2

It was young Sir Marstig that home from sea did fare ;
She would not rise, his own dear wife, nor give him greeting
    there.

3

It was young Sir Marstig that entered in apace ;
She would not rise, his own dear wife, nor look him in the
    face.

4

Still he stood, Sir Marstig, and thought right heavily :
"What ails her then, mine own dear wife, that hath no word
    for me ?"

5

"When thou didst depart, my husband, I was a knightly
    dame ;
Now am I queen in Denmark—the greater is my shame.

6

"Never again shalt slumber all on my lily-white arm,
Until thou hast slain King Erik, that wrought me dule and
    harm !"

7

It was young Sir Marstig that rode away to the Thing ;
Never a word he answered, until he should meet with the
    King.

8

It was young Sir Marstig stood forth in all men's sight,
He greeted there both page and squire and many a noble
    knight.

9

Up he stood, King Erik, and took him by the hand :
" Welcome now, Sir Marstig, home to lord and land ! "

10

Up and spake Sir Marstig, and wrathful was his mind :
" Oh, little I guessed when I fared forth what falsehood I left
    behind !

11

" Both Revel and Riga I won for thee, and that with mickle
    strife,
While thou, King Erik, didst bide at home to ravish my fair
    young wife ! "

12

" Harken now, Sir Marstig, and be not wroth with me !
Seven castles in Sælland, all will I give to thee."

13

" Seven castles in Sælland will never 'suage my shame ;
Know thou, King of Denmark, dearer I hold my dame !

14

" Harken, King of Denmark, and heed the words I say :
No fealty shalt thou have of me until my dying day ! "
—The lady she sits in Sælland, and weeps right woefully.

VIII

THE LONG BALLAD OF SIR MARSK STIG
(*Extract*)

35

Sɪʀ Mᴀʀsᴛɪɢ has donned his armour of proot
    And ridden away to the Thing,
With his merry men well weaponed in steel,
    All for to seek the King :
—My noble lord, the young Sir Marstig.

36

It was young Sir Marstig
    Before the Thing stood forth ;
He greeted the redesmen of the realm
    And the nobles of the north.

37

Sir Marstig stood in open Thing,
    And thus did speak and say :
" Because my wife hath suffered wrong
    Do I stand here to-day.

38

" Oh, I fared forth to a far countrie
    And risked for the realm my life—
Thou satst at home, King Erik,
    To ravish my fair young wife ! "

39

Up spake young King Erik,
    And smiled 'neath cloak of vair :
" Oh, her consent and will thereto
    As good as mine they were ! "

40

Up he spake, Sir Marstig,
  In mood that needs must mourn :
" Oh, well we wot the ancient saw
  That scathe must follow scorn.

41

" Now thou hast ravished my fair young wife
  A mock o' me to make,
But wot thou wilt, King Erik,
  I'll slay thee for her sake ! "

42

It was young Sir Marstig
  That turned him from the Thing :
" Bear witness, redesmen of the realm,
  That I defy the King ! "

43

" Now lithe and list, Sir Marstig,
  And let such prating be !
Castles and holds and lands so green
  All will I give to thee."

44

" Oh, little reck I of holds or lands,
  They ne'er shall 'suage my shame !
I would that the wrong had ne'er been wrought
  Against my dainty dame ! "

45

" Oh, Marstig, never so fast canst ride,
  But I can ride faster still ;
But wilt thou be mine enemy
  Then follow thy wasteful will ! "

46

"Oh, let my riding be ne'er so slow,
　　And ne'er so mild my mind,
Yet have we seen a small greyhound
　　Run down both hart and hind.

47

"Only do thou remember
　　The cause I have had to plead ;
Oft haps it that a hillock small
　　Doth throw a mighty steed !"

．　　．　　．　　．　　．　　．

86

Now when Sir Marstig slew the King
　　Little he rued the deed !
Forth he fared to Skanderborg
　　All on his swiftest steed.

87

It was she, the Queen o' Danes,
　　Forth from the window spied :
"Oh, yonder I see the self-made King
　　That to our hold doth ride !"

88

"Nay, never a self-made King am I
　　For all thy words, I ween ;
That name befits Drost Lovmand,
　　Lay last thine arms between.

89

"Oh, little to thee King Erik's death,
　　And less thy dule and pine,
So long as he lives, Drost Lovmand,
　　And thou dost hold him thine !"

90

Up spake young Prince Christopher,
  Clad all in the scarlet red :
"Oh, little amends, I wot, ye make
  For my father fallen and dead !"

91

Up he stood, Prince Christopher,
  And spake a royal word :
"Shalt get thee gone from out the realm
  If I am King and lord !"

92

"And must I depart from Denmark
  To sail the sea so deep,
So many a widow will I make
  That the noblest dames shall weep !

93

"And must I go a-roaming
  From wife and bairn, O King,
Denmark shall feel my foot, I trow,
  Both winter and summer and spring !"

.   .   .   .   .   .

95

It was young Sir Marstig,
  Home to his hold did fare ;
It was beauteous Ingeborg
  Came forth to meet him there.

96

Up spake young Sir Marstig,
  And held her in his arm :
"Now have I slain King Erik
  That wrought thee hurt and harm !

97

"Now wilt thou follow an outlawed man
  To dwell a landless dame,
Rather than be a light o' love,
  And bear the King his name?"

98

"Oh, rather I'd follow an outlawed man
  To dwell a Danish dame,
Than I would be a light o' love
  And bear the King his name!"

.   .   .   .   .   .

100

Oh, they have builded a hold at Hjælm,
  A hold with tower and wall,
Not to be won with engine of war,
  By arrow nor cannon-ball.[1]

101

Forth to his field went the farmer
  All for to sow his corn:
"Now help us, God in heaven above,
  Since Hjælm hath gotten a horn!"

102

Marstig he builded a hold at Hjælm,
  A hold with wall and tower;
The King in vain laid siege thereto
  With all his royal power.
—My noble lord, the young Sir Marstig.

---

[1] Cannons (bösser) are first mentioned in the time of Valdemar Atterdag (1340–85), and were certainly not known when Hjælm was besieged by Erik Mœndved. Their mention here is a proof that the Long Ballad was put together some hundred years after the event.

IX

NIELS EBBESON

Niels Ebbeson was the man of his hour ; and the hour was one of the blackest in Danish history. The worthless King Christopher was dead, his son Valdemar abroad, and the greedy Holstein nobles were scrambling for the choicest parts of the kingdom. One of these local tyrants, Count Gert, or Gerhardt, held Fyn and Jutland in pledge ; and how the Jutlanders found deliverance is best told by a Franciscan chronicler, writing in 1385 :

"Count Gerhardt of Holstein was then (Jan. 1340) in Lubeck. He heard tidings that his sister's son, Count of Sleswik, had made agreement with the Danes that they should establish the aforesaid Valdemar (V. Atterdag, King Christopher's son) in the kingdom, and marry him to Hedvig, the Duke's sister. Moreover, the Count knew well that many nobles and cities would fain, for the sake of peace, have a King in the land. . . . Count Gerhardt sent far and wide for help, and there came to him much people. . . . He invaded North Jutland. . . . Not long thereafter the Count fell sick in Randers. . . . It was his custom, when he was able, to sit up at night with his chaplain, and keep the Hours like a priest. When the Danes learnt his whereabouts, sixty doughty karls assembled, came to Randers on Thursday night (April 1, 1340) and, as though they were the night-watch for the sleeping army, took possession of a stone house. When the Count had read his Hours and lain down again, they came and struck him dead in his bed, with his chaplain and three pages. This heard a renowned knight from Westphalia, Henrik von Vitinghof, whose lodging was hard by : he came forth and attacked them, but they escaped, each his own way, without hurt. The foreign men-at-arms are much to be blamed for defending their lord so ill ; and they were forced with shame and scathe to return to the far countries whence they came."

We learn from other sources that the patriots fired a house to divert the Germans' attention, and that they escaped over Randers Bridge, which—having previously loosened the timbers—they broke down behind them. Thus they, and their leader Niels Ebbeson, saved Denmark from becoming a German province.

Little or nothing, apart from this exploit, is known of Niels Ebbeson ; his very dwelling-place, " Noringsris "—" Norroway " in one version of his Ballad—is unidentified. He and two of his brothers fell, fighting against the Holsteiners, at Skanderborg, on November 1, 1340 ; and their bodies were taken to the family burial-place in Vestervig monastic church.

Three noble families claimed him ; but recent researches have proved that he belonged to the Strangesons, chieftains in Ty, and descendants of Ebbe Skammelson (see No. 11), which family played a prominent part during the first half of the fourteenth century. They were connected by blood and intermarriage with another clan of

E

Strangesons, with the Frosters, Ove Haas, Niels Bugge, and the Globes of Vendesyssel. (This Ove Haas was a partisan of Count Gerhardt's, and fell at Randers.) In the opening dialogue of the Ballad the Count hints at Ebbeson's rumoured complicity with Bugge, leader of the rebellion, and tries generally to discover the attitude of Niels' powerful connections. With the latter's defence of Anders Frost, the trial of wits becomes a quarrel—for here the German and Danish systems of fealty are brought into collision.

The services of the vassal, by German law, belonged from birth to his liege lord, with whose consent alone could the contract be broken ; whereas the Danish chieftainship was based on the Law of Commutation, which gave the vassal the annual right to "take leave" (Orlov tage) and serve another chieftain. Twice over in the Ballad does Ebbeson gives his "swains" the choice whether or no they will follow him into danger ; and twice over the system of free-will service is vindicated by their answer.

Valiant attempts have been made by Danish antiquaries to identify "Swain Trøst"—Vedel, for instance, provided him with a name and a family—just as their English confrères would fain find an original for Robin Hood. But this Trusty Page had no local habitation : his very name is borrowed from the Ballad of Young Danneved ; for the Svend Trøst who saves his lord at a pinch is a figure frequently found in the ballad-world. Popular imagination, through him, does honour to all his class.

This Ballad is obviously the work of a minstrel (not contemporary with Niels), and is not associated with the Dance.

The Revised Conclusion is by another hand, and slightly later in date than the original version. A third exists, very imperfectly preserved, which is more historically accurate than either. It replaces Anders Frost by Esge, his father, and depicts Niels as asking aid of his brother Knud Ebbeson of Bygholm. We learn from it—with regret— that Niels' speech to his house-carles, and Swain Trøst's achievement, are the inventions of an admiring posterity.

One other poetical pæan must be quoted—the song-burst of a grave chronicler :

> "M semel et ter C bis binos X lege per te.
> Danorum mentes beat ipse dies Sitientes !
> Filius Ebbonis Nicholaus more leonis
> stravit serpentem Gerardum bella gerentem."

IX

NIELS EBBESON, 1340

1

THE Count to Denmark took his way,
  Nor failed for fear of strife,
Tho' langsyne 'twas to him foretold
  He there should lose his life.

2

Was none that might gainsay his will
  His fate to put to test ;
Yeoman and boor and knight and knave,
  With all he will be guest.

3

The Count he called Niels Ebbeson
  To come and meet with him,
And truce he sent him therewithal,
  And safety for life and limb.

4

The Count he met Niels Ebbeson
  Northward beside the sea :
"Now be thou welcome, Niels Ebbeson,
  Right welcome unto me !

5

" Blithe is thy cheer, Niels Ebbeson,
  Retainer dear of mine !
Say, what is the mind of the northern Jutes,
  And what of kinsmen thine ? "

6

" Oh, kinsmen have I 'mid the northern Jutes,
    And my wife hath kin alsò ;
And all of them shall do thy will,
    If they thy will may know."

7

" Niels Ebbeson, thou art a valiant man,
    And a man of wit beside,
And canst thou not ride straightforward,
    The long way round thou'lt ride.

8

" Now lithe and listen, Niels Ebbeson,
    Wilt thou mine errand speed,
Then say how many swains hast thou
    Will stand thee by at need ? "

9

" Oh, five and forty carles have I,
    Such as they well may be ;
And be they many or be they few
    Right dear are they to me."

10

" And hast thou five and forty carles
    Well art thou served, I ween !
But last night wert thou in Sir Bugge's hold
    With a hundred mail-clad men."

11

Niels Ebbeson he stamped his foot,
    And straight made answer high :
" Is any man here, or knight or knave,
    Who dares maintain that lie ?

12

"Is any man here, or knight or knave,
    Dares put it to the touch,
Never a foot will I give back,
    For I have sworn as much!"

13

"Lithe and listen, Niels Ebbeson,
    Such words must have an end!
Now seek him, and see, Sir Bugge,
    If he will be my friend.

14

"Sir Bugge and Povl Glob the young
    To do my will did swear,
And Sir Anders Frost is one with them,
    And foremost in counsel there.

15

"And more have sworn to do my will
    That now will work me woe;
So list and heed Sir Bugge's rede,
    And see how the thing will go!"

16

"Oh, nought know I of Sir Bugge's mind,
    What he may say or do;
But Anders hath kept his faith with thee,
    As all men will tell thee true.

17

"Anders hath kept his faith with thee,
    As all men will tell thee true;
But, would he take leave of thy service,
    Such leave is a free man's due.

18

"For this is the Danish custom,
  And hath been from days of yore,
If a swain would cease his service,
  He should have leave therefor."

19

Up and spake Sir Gert the Count
  That liked his words right ill :
"Oh, never a vassal should leave his lord
  Save with his lord's good-will !"

20

"Oh, none is joined with a holy vow
  Save a monk to his cowl of grey !
Let chieftains come and chieftains go,
  Men serve them as best they may !"

21

"Overbold is his speech, Niels Ebbeson,
  Dares bandy words with me !
Or thou shalt depart from Denmark
  Or I'll hang thee to a tree !"

22

"And must I depart from Denmark,
  From wife's and bairn's embrace,
Oh, thou shalt call it a luckless hour
  That ever thou saw'st my face !"

23

"Get hence, get hence, Niels Ebbeson,
  Let all thy prating be !
Or I will do what well I may,
  And break my truce with thee !"

24

"Oh, ne'er hast thou seen me so sore afraid
　　As to tremble for curse and ban !
Look well to thyself, Lord Count, I say,
　　And defend thy head like a man !"

25

"Niels Ebbeson, thy words are wild,
　　To hold thy peace were best ;
But I will keep truce with thee to-day
　　Till the sun goes down to rest."

26

Niels Ebbeson waved his lily-white hand,
　　And turned his steed on the shore :
"Farewell, Count Gert, with all thy men !
　　Soon shall we meet once more."

27

Niels Ebbeson he fled full fast,
　　Nor spur was fain to spare,
And the Count held back with all his men,
　　Was none durst follow there.

28

It was he, Niels Ebbeson,
　　That to his hold did win ;
It was his own dear lady
　　Came forth to lead him in.

29

"Now lithe and listen, mine own dear wife,
　　And my rede shall rise at thee ;
The Count will drive me from the land
　　Or hang me to a tree !"

30

"What counsel can I give to thee
  That have but a woman's wit?
The worst of rede were here the best
  Could we but light on it.

31

"The worst of rede were here the best,
  All in this evil hour,
Either the Count to strike adown
  Or burn him in his bower!

32

"Now let thy steeds to the smithy fare
  (This is my counsel true),
And see that their shoon turn the backward way
  When they are shod anew.

33

"Oh, see that their shoon turn the backward way,
  So the foemen thy track shall miss,
And take heed and tell to no man
  That a woman taught thee this!"

34

Up and spake Niels Ebbeson,
  Unto his men cried he:
"Now which of you will follow,
  And which take leave of me?

35

"Let him that now will follow
  Stretch forth his hand to me,
And he that now will take his leave
  Speak up right speedilie!"

36

Up they stood, his Danish squires,
   And answered their lord so free :
"Lo, all of us will follow
   And risk our lives for thee ! "

37

Oh, up they rode to Lady-wood,
   And there their steeds did bind,
And forth into the town they went
   Count Gert to seek and find.

38

It was he, Niels Ebbeson,
   To Randers Bridge did ride :
"Now let him take leave and go his way
   Dares not the brunt abide ! "

39

Up and spake he, little boy Trust,
   More faithful than them all :
"Now give me leave, my master,
   And saddle and steed withal ! "

40

He gave him leave, his master,
   And saddle and steed withal,
And or ever the day was over
   He served him best of all.

41

It was he, Niels Ebbeson,
   With sword that smote the door :
"Stand up, stand up, Lord Gert the Count,
   For thou shalt sleep no more !

42

"Stand up, Lord Gert the Count,
   And lend to me thine ear,
Duke Henrik's messenger am I,
   And he hath sent me here.

43

"Harken, Gert the Count,
   Nor longer lay thee down !
Kolding is beleaguered,
   And burnt is Ribe town."

44

"And dost thou tell me tidings true,
   Then good are such tidings to hear ;
Forth from the hold while yet we live,
   And forth with the steeds and gear !"

45

Oh, they have opened wide the door
   That the message might be sped,
And it was he, Niels Ebbeson,
   Went up to the County's bed.

46

"Oh, thou and I, Niels Ebbeson,
   Can a better bargain strike ;
Word will we send to Duke Henrik
   And Sir Klaus Krummerdike."

47

"Yestere'en thy words were other,
   All out upon the strand ;
I should go to the gallows,
   Or get me from the land."

48

Up and spake the swarthy swain :
　"Now waste no further word !
Let be, let be thy tedious tale,
　And harken to the sword ! "

49

They've seized him, Gert the Count,
　All by his golden hair,
And they have hewn his neck in twain
　Over his bedside there.

50

Now when the Count was done to death
　All on their drums they beat ;
Forth he fared, Niels Ebbeson,
　And galloped adown the street.

51

Forth he fared, Niels Ebbeson,
　And fain would flee away,
But there he met Sir Ove Haas
　That strove to say him nay.

52

"Now lithe and listen, Sir Ove Haas,
　And see that thou let me go,
For thou hast wed my kinswoman,
　And that thou well dost know."

53

"And have I wed thy kinswoman,
　Then kin am I to thee,
But since thou hast struck down my lord
　I may not let thee be ! "

54

Niels Ebbeson drew his brand so brown,
　　For ne'er would he shrink from strife ;
Sir Ove and many a Teuton swain
　　Must there lay down his life.

55

It was he, Niels Ebbeson,
　　To Randers Bridge did ride,
And the little page that erst took leave
　　Was standing there beside.

56

Niels Ebbeson rode o'er the bridge,
　　For fast his foes came on ;
It was the little foot-page
　　That broke the bridge adown.

57

Niels Ebbeson rode to Noringsris,
　　And fast he spurred his steed,
Sore, good sooth, was his anguish,
　　And sore, good sooth, his need.

58

She sheltered him, an old good-wife,
　　Of loaves that had but two,
And she's given one to Niels Ebbeson
　　Because the Count he slew !

THE RE-MODELLED CONCLUSION OF NIELS EBBESON

34

"Now eat ye, and drink, my Danish squires,
  And see that your hearts be gay !
For when the night is overpast
  Oh, then we will seize the day.

35

"When day doth dawn and sun doth shine
  We shall have tidings new ;
And then shall I see, 'mid all my men,
  How many will stand me true."

36

Up they stood, the Danish squires,
  And answered their lord so free :
"Oh, we will risk both goods and life
  And all to ride with thee ! "

37

Oh, up they rode to Lady-wood,
  And there their steeds they bind,
And in they've gone to Randers town,
  Count Gert to seek and find.

38

Forth he fared, Niels Ebbeson,
  To Randers Bridge came he :
"Now let him take leave and go his way
  That will not follow me ! "

39

Up they stood, the captains good,
  Swore fealty to their lord anew,
All but Niels Ebbeson's sister's son,
  Was there to him untrue.

40

It was he, Niels Ebbeson,
  With sword that smote the door :
"Stand up, stand up, Sir Gert the Count,
  For thou shalt sleep no more !

41

"Stand up, stand up, Sir Gert the Count,
  And lend to me thine ear !
Duke Henrik's messenger am I,
  And he hath sent me here."

42

"And art thou Duke Henrik's messenger,
  Then tarry thou not too long ;
To-morrow we'll meet in the Greyfriars' Kirk
  'Twixt Mass and Evensong."

43

"Stand up, Sir Gert the Count,
  Nor longer lay thee down !
Kolding is beleaguered,
  And burnt is Ribe town !"

44

Forth from the window looked the Count,
  And the shining spears he spied :
"Oh, luckless the hour that I came in !
  Niels Ebbeson holds outside."

45

They knocked at the door with glaive and with spear,
    That loosed were lock and link :
"Art thou within, Lord Gert the Count,
    A health to thee we'll drink !"

46

"Now set thee down upon my bed,
    A league we can form, belike ;
Word will we send to Duke Henrik,
    And Sir Klaus Krummerdike."

47

"Oh, neither keep nor hold have I
    To guard so rich a prey !
Draw out, draw out the swords so sharp,
    And let them have their way !"

48

The goose did cackle, the sheep did bleat,
    And the cock in the high loft crew ;
'Twas by daylight and not in darkness
    That Gert the Count they slew.

49

God rest thy soul, Niels Ebbeson,
    All for that slaying's sake !
Full many a German in Denmark
    The self-same way shall take.

LEGENDARY BALLADS

X

HAVBOR AND SIGNELIL

THE story of Havbor, or Hagbard, and Signe-lil is a very ancient one. Sven Grundtvig gives it a Russian origin ; but, however that may be, it is traced back by other Danish authorities to the dim period of Folk-Migration, before the Skjoldung kings. Sung in an antique Lay— which has perished — it was re-told by Saxo Grammaticus, and frequently referred to in the works of the Icelandic skalds between the ninth and eleventh centuries. The twelfth-century Kormak's Saga mentions a representation of Hagbard among the carvings in Thorkel's hall. Snorris' Edda (Skaldskarparsmal) gives Hagbard's name in a list of sea-kings ; and Brynhild (Vol-sunga Saga 25) calls him the first of men before the birth of Sigurd Fafnirsbane.

The probable scene of the tragedy is Sigarsted, in Sjælland, near Ringsted, the ancient royal residence. There the sites yet exist of Sigar's palace and Signe's bower — there, too, is the howe where the gibbet was raised, and the field where Sigar was defeated by Hagbard's avenging kinsmen. They were visited by Ole Worm in 1642, and a map of them was published in *Monumenta Danica*. The Rev. S. M. Beyer, in 1791, excited the antiquarian world by his alleged discovery of a rune-stone commemorating King Sigar—but, since the stone, he was careful to add, had since been destroyed, the statement, to put it mildly, lacks verification.

The ballad-minstrel omits much of the original story, but adds details of his own—Havbor's reply to the serving-maid, the King's remorseful outburst, and the punishment of the tale-bearer. The binding of Havbor with Signe's hair, and his refusal to break it, though appearing at first sight a touch of fantastic mediæval chivalry, probably harks back to a much more primitive superstition, well known to all witches — that which regards the hair as enshrining the life of its possessor. In verse 20 we have a faint reminiscence of the antique Shield-Maidens, Choosers of the Slain.

X

HAVBOR AND SIGNELIL

1

Havbor the King and Sivord the King
  Have fallen out in strife,
All for the stately Signelil
  That was so fair a wife.
—Ne'er wilt thou win such a fair one.

2

Havbor the King he dreamt a dream,
  And woeful did he wake;
He went to seek his mother,
  And unto her he spake:

3

"Methought that I was up in heaven,
  And that was so fair a town;
And I held proud Signelil in mine arms,
  And we fell from the sky adown."

4

"And didst thou dream thou wast in heaven,
  And fellest adown from the sky,
That bodes that thou wilt win the maid,
  But for her sake shalt die!"

5

"And if I win the maiden
  Such happiness have I,
I count the cost but little
  That I for her must die!"

6

Havbor he let his locks wax long,
    And clad him in woman's gear,
And so he rode to Denmark
    As though he maiden were.

7

All in the midst of the castle garth
    His garment changed he,
Then entered in the ladies' bower
    Proud Signelil to see.

8

"Here sittest thou, stately Signelil,
    With matrons and maids arow!
Havbor hath sent me hither
    To learn to broider and sew."

9

"All the woman's craft I know
    Shall be for thee displayed;
Shalt eat from the self-same dish as I,
    And sleep with my serving-maid."

10

"Oh, I have eaten with king's children,
    And lain in their arms at night;
And must I sleep with thy serving-maid
    I shall die of the sore despite."

11

"Now lithe and listen, my beauteous maid,
    Let all thy sorrow be!
Shalt eat of the self-same dish as I,
    And sleep by the side of me."

12

He's taken out a knife so small,
   And cut as best he could ;
He's shaped them out, both hind and hart,
   That run in good greenwood.

13

Still sat all the haughty maids
   And sewed as best they might,
All save Havbor, the son of kings,
   His needle still did bite.

14

Up and spake the serving-maid,
   So evil a tongue had she :
"Oh, never saw I so poor a seam
   Sewn by a fair ladye !

15

"Ever her needle is in her mouth,
   She sets no stitches fine ;
And ever she drains the goblet out,
   So deep as they pour the wine !

16

"Ne'er have I seen a lady's hands
   Stiffer than steel, I trow !
And ne'er have I seen so bold an eye
   Under a lady's brow ! "

17

"Now hold thy tongue, thou evil maid,
   And speak no spite of me !
Let me turn mine eyes where'er I may
   I'll turn them not on thee ! "

18

Now all were bound to slumber,
   Whenas the eve was spent ;
Havbor and stately Signelil
   To the self-same chamber went.

19

She laid her hand on Havbor's breast
   That shone with gold so red :
"Why hast thou a bosom so like a man,
   And not the breasts of a maid ?"

20

"Oh, the custom it is in my father's land
   That maids to the Thing should fare,
And therefore have I no maiden's breasts
   Because of the mail we wear !

21

"Now tell me, stately Signelil,
   While we are all alone,
Is there ever a man in all the world
   Thou hast set thy heart upon ?"

22

"Oh, there's never a man in all the world
   That lies my heart within,
Saving young Havbor, the son of kings,
   That I may never win."

23

"And is it Havbor, the son of kings,
   That to thy heart is dear,
Then turn thee hither, mine own true love !
   He is sleeping all so near !"

24

"And art thou Havbor, the son of kings?
  Why hast thou shamèd me?
Why didst not ride to my father's court
  With hawk on hand so free?"

25

"Oh, how should I ride with hawk on hand
  To thy father's court so free?
Full well I know thy wrathful sire
  Would hang me to a tree!"

26

"Now hush thee, hush thee, Havbor,
  And take thou heed, I pray!
My serving-maid lies waking
  And listens to all we say."

27

"Oh, let her lie and listen,
  Thine evil serving-maid!
Beneath my bolster are hidden
  Both corselet and trusty blade.

28

"Beneath my bolster are hidden
  Both corselet and sword so true;
And were a hundred warriors here
  The meeting they should rue!"

29

Oh, she has heard their counsel,
  The evil serving-maid;
She's stolen away his byrnie brown
  But and his trusty blade.

30

Both trusty blade and byrnie brown
   She's secretly stolen away ;
She's hied her to the chamber fair
   Where Sivord the King he lay.

31

"Oh, sleep ye, wake ye, my noble lord ?
   Your slumber is all too deep !
For now lies Havbor, the son of kings,
   By your daughter's side asleep."

32

"Now hold thy peace, thou evil maid,
   For an thou art a liar,
To-morrow or ever the sun goes down
   Thou shalt be burnt with fire ! "

33

"Lithe now and listen, King Sivord,
   Well may ye trust my word ;
For here is Havbor's byrnie brown
   But and his trusty sword."

34

Up he sprang, King Sivord,
   And cried thro' bower and hall :
"Rise up, rise up, my merry men,
   And don your armour all !

35

"Now don your mail, my merry men,
   And clasp it well enough,
For here is Havbor, the son of kings,
   A warrior tall and tough ! "

36

Oh, they have knocked at the chamber door
 With glaive and eke with spear :
" Rise up now, Havbor, son of kings !
 Come forth and meet us here ! "

37

Up sprang Havbor, the son of kings,
 Or ever they spake the word,
And he has missed his byrnie brown,
 But and his trusty sword.

38

" Oh, gone, gone is my byrnie,
 And gone my blade so true !
Now by my troth, proud Signelil,
 This meeting we shall rue ! "

39

All hail to Havbor, son of kings,
 That fought like a warrior stout !
Ne'er could his foes come nigh him
 While the boards of the bed held out.

40

Oh, some he slew with his naked hands,
 And some underfoot did tread ;
Full thirty of King Sivord's men
 By Signild's bower lay dead.

41

They've taken Havbor, the son of kings,
 And fetters on him they draw ;
He burst them all asunder
 As they had been of straw.

42

Oh, shame be on the serving-maid
    That gave them counsel there :
"Never shall ye bind Havbor
    But with proud Signild's hair ! "

43

They took a hair of Signild's head
    To bind him foot and hand ;
His haughty heart had broken
    Ere he would burst that band.

44

"Now harken, haughty Signelil !
    Wilt show thy love to me,
Then burn thy bower and all therein
    When they hang me to a tree ! "

45

"Oh, is there a man of my father's men
    That in thy death hath part,
Be sure I will avenge it
    All on his own sweetheart ! "

46

Up spake Havbor, the son of kings,
    When first he saw the tree :
"Hang up my cloak of scarlet
    A sign for all to see !

47

"Hang up my cloak of scarlet
    That is both fair and fine !
The ladies all will weep and wail
    When first they see the sign."

48

It was stately Signelil
　To roof and reed set fire ;
She and all her maidens
　Burned in the self-same pyre.

49

Long stood Havbor, the son of kings,
　To look his last on land,
Until he saw proud Signild's bower
　That all in flame did stand.

50

"Take down, take down my cloak of red,
　And cast it to earth so deep,
For an I had ten thousand lives
　Not one of them would I keep ! "

51

Up and spake King Sivord,
　That looked, and needs must speak :
"Oh, what is the bale a-burning there,
　But and the driving reek ? "

52

Up and spake the little foot-page,
　And sore his tears ran down :
"Oh, that is stately Signelil
　That lets her love be shown ! "

53

"Save her, stately Signelil !
　See that ye ride and run !
Get ye in haste to the gallows
　And save King Havbor's son ! "

54

When they came to the bower
   Signelil's soul was sped ;
When they came to the gallows
   Havbor was hanged and dead.

55

"Oh, had I known but yesternight
   How deep in love were they,
I would not ha' done for all Denmark
   The deed I ha' done this day ! "

56

Now woe is me for the gallows-tree,
   And the bower in ashes laid !
They've buried her in the earth alive,
   The cruel serving-maid.
—Ne'er wilt thou win such a fair one.

XI

EBBE SKAMMELSON

THIS ballad of a brother's treachery (which may
be compared with our own "Childe Vyet ") dates
from *circa* 1300, and is considered by Olrik as the
best produced in Denmark during the mediæval
period.   In character-drawing it yields to none.
Proud Adelus, "strong in will and true in troth,"
is the ideal noble lady ; the hot-blooded hero, the
cowardly brother, and the mother with her un-

availing attempt at smoothing things over, are all well individualized. The burden, too, is peculiarly haunting and picturesque.

Tradition points to the Nordentoft homestead in North Jutland (Ty) as the scene of the tragedy ; and the great Strangeson family claims Ebbe as its founder.

XI

EBBE SKAMMELSON

1

Skammel he dwells up north in Ty,
　And Skammel is rich and gay ;
Five sons hath he both fair and tall,
　But two went an evil way.
—Therefore roams Ebbe Skammelson so many
　a lonely way.

2

Sir Ebbe serves for fame and fee
　The royal court within,
While Peter his brother that bides at home
　His true-love's troth would win.

3

"Dost sit at home, proud Adelus,
　And broider my brother's gear ?
Ebbe he serves in the King's own court,
　And scorns thee, nor holds thee dear !"

4

" Full well do I know him, Ebbe,
   And Ebbe his heart knows he ;
And scorns he never a maiden proud
   The less hath he scorn for me ! "

5

" Now lithe and listen, proud Adelus,
   And be my plighted maid !
For true I tell thee the tidings
   That Ebbe my brother is dead."

6

All on the self-same evening
   They drank to the plighted pair ;
All on the Monday after
   To bridal-feast they fare.

7

It was Ebbe Skammelson
   At midnight did awake,
And he up and called to the nearest swain
   And of his dream he spake.

8

" Methought that my stone-built tower
   Stood all in a leaping lowe,
And Peter my brother burned therein,
   And my fair love alsò."

9

" And didst thou dream thy tower of stone
   Stood all in a lowe so red,
Then know, that Peter thy brother
   Thine own fair love doth wed."

10

It was Ebbe Skammelson
  That girt his sword by his side,
And leave he won, Sir Ebbe,
  Homeward in haste to ride.

11

It was Ebbe Skammelson
  That paused not on his way ;
He came to his father's castle
  All on the bridal-day.

12

Forth they come, his sisters twain,
  With bracelets on either hand :
"Now welcome, Ebbe our brother,
  Home to thy father's land !"

13

"Now lithe and listen, my sisters twain,
  And look that ye do not lie !
Say wherefore are gathering hither
  This goodly companie ?"

14

Up spake his youngest sister,
  For needs must the words be said :
"Lo ! 'tis Peter thy brother
  Thine own true-love doth wed !"

15

To one he has given a brooch for her breast,
  To the other a ring for her hand :
"Oh, I brought them both to my own true-love
  Out of the strangers' land !"

16

The one she has bidden him bide at home,
   The other has bidden him go :
" For dost thou tarry here o'er this night
   Be sure it will work us woe ! "

17

Ebbe he turned his horse's head
   Forth from the hold to ride,
But his mother she seized the bridal-rein
   And begged him at home to bide.

18

His mother all to the highest place
   Hath brought him cushion and chair,
His father hath brought him a cup of wine
   To pledge the bridal-pair.

19

He pledged them in the mead so brown
   And in the red, red wine,
But when he looked upon the bride
   The tears ran from his eyne.

20

Now when the dew was falling
   And even was well-nigh sped,
Up she rose, the beauteous bride,
   To seek the bridal-bed.

21

They followed her, the beauteous bride,
   All to her chamber door ;
Foremost went Ebbe Skammelson
   To hold the torch before.

2 2

All to the door of the upper room
  Ebbe the bride led he :
" Hast thou forgot, proud Adelus,
  The troth thou didst plight to me ? "

2 3

" All the troth I plighted thee
  Is given to Peter thy brother ;
But each and every day I live
  I'll be to thee e'en as a mother ! "

2 4

" I wooed thee not for my mother,
  I wooed thee for my wife !
For this shall Peter Skammelson
  Yield up to me his life !

2 5

" Lithe and listen, proud Adelus,
  And fly from the land with me !
Peter my brother I'll slay eftsoon,
  And bear the blame for thee."

2 6

" And wilt thou slay Peter thy brother eftsoon
  I never will be thy wage !
And thou shalt sorrow thyself to death
  Like a wild bird in a cage."

2 7

It was Ebbe Skammelson
  That drew his brand so brown ;
It was haughty Adelus
  That he to earth struck down.

G

28

Oh, he has hidden the bloody brand
    Beneath his cloak of pall ;
He's sought his brother Sir Peter
    That sat in the stone-built hall.

29

"Now harken, Peter Skammelson,
    A laggard art thou to wed !
The bride is longing after thee
    All in the bridal-bed."

30

It was Peter his brother
    Spake up with mickle spite :
"I give thee leave with right good-will
    To sleep by the bride to-night !"

31

It was Ebbe Skammelson
    That drew his brand so brown ;
It was Peter his brother
    That he to earth struck down.

32

Oh, he has wounded his father sore,
    And struck off his mother's hand ;
And so must he roam, Ebbe Skammelson,
    The wild ways of the land !
—Therefore roams Ebbe Skammelson so many a
    lonely way.

XII, XIII
OH, SEVENTY-SEVEN TWICE-TOLD
WERE THEY
HOLGER DANSKE AND STOUT DIDRIK

THESE Ballads are two of a large group cele-
brating popular legendary heroes. Those concerned with Didrik—all jovial ones with happy
endings—were adapted or translated from the
work of the wandering German minstrels known
as the "Saxon Singers," who visited Denmark
during the time of Knud Lavard and Sven Grade
(1131–57). Part of this poetry, moreover, apparently trickled into Scandinavia by circuitous
routes, since a lengthy "Didrikssaga" was composed during the thirteenth century at Bergen.

There are those who consider Didrik as a mere
Mrs. Harris, and derive his name from the vague
appellation *þioðreke* = folk-king. But most authorities believe that he had a flesh-and-blood original
in Theoderic, King of the East Goths, and con-
queror of Italy, whose royal seat was at " Bern,"
i. e. Verona. Be that as it may, this kingly shade
enlisted his champions among the most august
phantoms of the North. Sivord Snarensvend, for
example, is no less a personage than Sigurd
Fafnirsbane ; while Helled Haagen is Hogne the
Hero, Sigurd's slayer. Raadengaard may (or may

not) be the Hrothgar of "Beowulf," and the "Sir Aldingar" of British ballad. Most of the other figures may be pursued through the mazes of legend ; but Falkvor the Fiddler is a creation of the "fiddling" minstrel's ; and he or his translator inserted Tetlev Danske as a compliment to the Danes.

As for Holger Danske, he is the French hero Ogier le Danois, originally one of Charlemagne's champions, who fought for Christendom against the infidel. The oldest Danish ballad of Holger describes his victory over Burmand, an amorous Troll, who would fain carry off the Lady Gloriant, the King of Hungary's daughter, from her rightful lover King Karvel. This chivalrous deed of Holger's captivated the popular fancy, which adopted him henceforth as national hero, crowned him with the "red, red gold" and pictured him as defending Denmark against the power of the German Empire, personified in the giants Sverting and Bermer-Ris. "Holger Danske and Stout Didrik may," says Olrik, "be considered Denmark's first patriotic song."

Verses 4 and 5 find a parallel in "The Battle of Otterburn" (English version).

> "Up spake a berne upon the bent
> Of comfort that was not cold,
> And said : We have brente Northumberland,
> We have all wealth in hold.

"Now we have harried all Bambroughshire,
  All the wealth in the world have we ;
I rede we ride to Newcastle
  So still and stalworthlie ! "

XII

OH, SEVENTY-SEVEN TWICE-TOLD
WERE THEY

1

Oh, seventy-seven twice-told were they
  When out from Hald they went,
And when they came to Brattingsborg
  They pitched the silken tent.
—There sounds thunder the captains under,
    when they ride forth.

2

King Isung stands on high watch-tower,
  And looks forth far and wide :
" Oh, little care for their lives have they
  That hither list to ride !

3

" Now harken, Sivord Snarensvend,
  Hast wandered here and there ;
Tell me what warriors are they
  These golden shields that bear ? "

4

" There shineth on the foremost shield
  A lion all so bold ;
The bearing of Didrik the King it is,
  With a crown of ruddy gold.

5

"And shining on the second shield
    Hammer and tongs appear;
The sign of Vidrik Verlandson
    That takes no prisoner.

6

"And on the third shield shining see
    A golden serpent, bound;
That beareth Master Hildebrand,
    Cunning in counsel found.

7

"And on the fourth shield, see where shines
    A leafy linden-tree;
That beareth youthful Humlunger,
    Earl Hornbook's son is he.

8

"There shineth on the following shield
    A wolf in a wild wood,
The sign of Ulv van Jærn the young
    Who is a warrior good.

9

"And on the sixth there shineth still
    A vulture red as gold;
And that bears Helled Haagen
    Who is a champion bold.

10

"And see, the seventh shining shield
    Fiddle and bow doth keep,
The sign of Falkvor Minstrel-Man
    Would liefer drink than sleep.

11

"And on the eighth an elephant
  Is pictured with a swain,
The sign of Tetlev Danske
  That swings his sword amain.

12

"All on the ninth shield shining, lo
  A swarthy vulture shows,
The sign of young Sir Raadengaard
  Full many a rune who knows.

13

"And on the tenth shield, lo there shine
  Two arrows wan and white,
He bears them, Hvitting Hermandson,
  Is foremost still in fight.

14

"There shines on the eleventh shield
  Nought but a burning brand ;
That bears Sir Brand Vidfærling
  Against all lordling's land.

15

"And on the twelfth shield shining, see,
  There stands a cowl so grey ;
That bears the monk, Brother Alsing,
  Would follow fain the fray ! "

16

"Now harken, Sivord Snarensvend,
  Thou art a warrior free !
Shalt fight with one of Didrik's men
  For all my land and me ! "

17

Up stood Sivord Snarensvend,
 And to the tents he hied:
"Now is there ever a warrior stout
 A joust with me will ride?"

18

Oh, on the board they cast the dice
 That fell both far and wide,
And the lot it was young Humlunger's
 With Sivord there to ride.

19

It was he, young Humlunger,
 Did forth to Vidrik speed:
"Now I will give thee a pledge to hold
 Wilt lend me Skemming thy steed."

20

"Oh, Sivord sees not the point of his spear,
 Because his sight is dim,
And if my Skemming to-day wins scathe
 Nor thou nor thy kinsfolk can pay for him!"

21

"But I, I have a sister
 Is fairer than maidens all;
And if thy Skemming wins scathe to-day
 I'll pay it her hand withal."

22

"Oh, nought of Skemming thou'lt see to-day
 Unless thy surety firm doth stand;
The hand I'll have of thy sister fair,
 And seven castles in Birtingsland!"

23

" Seven castles in Birtingsland
    Thy surety they shall be ;
Thereto the maid my sister,
    A pledge of price for thee ! "

24

Oh, he has backed that steed so bold,
    And gaily ridden away ;
Good sooth, but Skemming thought it strange
    To feel the spur that day !

25

The gold did shine upon his shield
    Like the sun in summer-tide :
" God help me now, a simple swain,
    The brunt to bear and bide ! "

26

The first course that they ran together
    Would neither champion yield ;
And both their shields were shattered there,
    And hurled so far afield.

27

" Methinks thou art a fair young swain,
    That well can run and ride !
Go now and take thy shield again,
    And I the brunt will bide."

28

And when they ran the second course,
    Then one of them must yield ;
Young Humlunger was stricken,
    And hurled so far afield.

29

"Oh, I have struck thee down to earth,
  And wounded thy steed alsò;
Now whence thou comest, thou fair young swain,
  Full fain am I to know."

30

"Oh, Hornbook hight my father,
  In Birtingsland is lord,
And I am called young Humlunger
  Whenas I ride abroad."

31

"Full well I know thy father,
  For comrades kind we were;
Now take thy shield and mount again,
  Son of my sister dear!

32

"And take thou up my shattered shield,
  Bind me to oaken tree;
Then ride and tell the champions
  The game is won by thee!"

33

Forth to the tents fared Humlunger,
  Cast blade upon the board:
"Now have I bound the grey-beard carle
  That spake the vaunting word!"

34

"Now hold thy peace, young Humlunger,
  That aye must prate thy fill!
If thou hast bound him, Sivord,
  'Tis with his own good-will!"

35

Up stood Vidrik Verlandson,
  Bade saddle his steed so free :
"I will fare forth to the forest,
  This conquered carle to see!"

36

Oh, Sivord all in the greenwood
  Saw where the knight did ride ;
Up by the roots he reft the oak,
  For he might not his bonds abide.

37

Up by the roots he reft the oak,
  For he might not his bonds abide :
"If Vidrik Verlandson comes here
  My ribs he'll hew from my side!"

38

The Queen stood in the lofty bower,
  And looked both up and down :
"Oh, hither comes Sivord Snarensvend
  A-bearing summer to town!"

39

The Queen looked out with her ladies
  All from the lofty bower :
"Sivord hath been in good greenwood
  And gathered a gallant flower!"

40

Gay went the dance at Brattingsborg,
  Where champions danced amain ;
There danced with oak-tree in his belt
  Sivord the purblind swain !
—There sounds thunder the captains under, when
    they ride forth.

XIII

HOLGER DANSKE AND STOUT DIDRIK

1

Stout Didrik dwells in Berneland
  With brethren eight all told,
And each of them twelve sons hath got,
  All doughty knights and bold.
—But the battle is raging northward up in Jutland.

2

Stout Didrik dwells in Berneland
  With fifteen sisters bright,
And each of them hath twelve fair sons
  That hold their lives full light.

3

And when they rode out all by Bern,
  A goodly companie,
Sooth to say, each warrior
  Was tall as a beechen tree.

4

" Now we have fought o'er all the world
  And conquered far and wide,
And we have heard of Holger Dansk
  That doth in Denmark bide.

5

" We have heard tell of Holger Dansk,
  In Jutland doth abide,
And he is crowned with the red, red gold,
  And ne'er will bate his pride."

6

Oh, Sverting seized a pike of steel,
  And spake up loud and high :
" A hundred of Holger Danske's men
  I count them not a fly ! "

7

" Oh, harken, Sverting, thou swarthy swain,
  Or ever thou rue the day !
We ha' heard of Holger Danske's men,
  And bold young blades are they ! "

8

Up and spake tall Bermer-Ris,
  And a vaunting word spake he :
" Oh, we will fare to Denmark,
  And try if the King will flee ! "

9

Now all with eighteen thousand steeds
  From Berneland they fare,
And they've drawn up to Denmark
  To see King Holger there.

10

Stout Didrik hath sent a messenger
  And bidden King Holger yield,
To pay him scot and lot for aye,
  Or meet him in the field.

11

Up spake Vidrik Verlandson,
  He spake a word so stout :
" And come they in to Denmark thus,
  They shall not thus go out ! "

12

Oh, they have met, a mighty host,
　All on the darksome heath ;
And that was a woeful trysting-place
　Where warriors fought till death.

13

They've fought for a day, for three they've fought,
　And stiff in stower they stand ;
Holger the King and his mighty men
　Slew many from Berneland.

14

Oh, mild of mood was Bermer-Ris,
　And softly spake he then :
" Now how shall we conquer Holger Dansk
　With scarce a hundred men ? "

15

It was doughty Didrik
　Looked upward to the sky :
" No help is here for us, I ween,
　'Tis time to turn and fly ! "

16

Stout Didrik took to both his legs,
　To fly o'er hill and dale,
And Sverting went the self-same way
　For all his boastful tale.

17

Up spake little Iron-Wolf,
　That held the hill beside :
" Oh, they that are come to fight the Danes
　Have little praise or pride ! "

18

When they rode out of Berneland
  They were eighteen thousand men ;
'Twas scarce a tithe of all that host
  That won back home again.

19

Oh, stern the stream of red, red blood
  Ran o'er land and lea !
The reek of it rose up to heaven
  Till the sun was bloody and red to see.
  But the battle is raging northward up in Jutland.

BALLADS OF MAGIC

XIV
YOUNG SVEJDAL

A CERTAIN number of Ballads borrowed their subjects from the Old Norse Lays, making of them, not translations, but fresh creations ; for the Lays tower above the many-coloured ballad-world like ice-peaks that loom over flowery meads. The story of Young Svejdal is derived from two Lays dealing with the adventures of Svipdag, who wakes Menglad from her trance on the magic mountain ; but

"there is a vast difference between the simplicity of the Ballad and the stately measure and rhetorical pomp of the original :—

' Svipdag is my name ; Sunbright was my father's name ;
  The winds have driven me far, along cold ways ;
  No one can gainsay the word of Fate,
  Though it be spoken to his own destruction.'

" The difference is as great as the difference between the ballad of the ' Marriage of Gawayne ' and the same story as told in the *Canterbury Tales ;* or the difference between Homer's way of describing the recovery of lifted cattle and the ballad of ' Jannie Telfer of the Fair Dodhead ' " (W. P. Ker's *Epic andRomance*, chap. ii., section 3).

This Ballad, indeed, brings down the story from the misty peaks of Valhalla into the garrulous region of fairy-tale. It is faithful to the primitive tradition which depicts the dead as waking unwillingly from their slumbers. Svejdal's mother speaks as does the dead Vala in the nameless Lay called " Baldr's Doom " by the editors of the *Corpus Poeticum Boreale*:

> " Hvat es manna þat mer okunnra
> es mer hefir aukit ervitt sinni ?
> Vas-ek snivin sniovi ok slegin regni,
> ok drifin doeggo ; dauð vas-ek lengi."

(Who is the man unknown to me that has put me to this weary journey? I was snowed on with snow, and smitten with rain, and dripped on with dew ; dead was I lang syne.)

The refrain is :

> " Nauðig sagðak. Nú mun-ek þegja ! "

(Loath have I spoken. Now must I be silent !) Gray, in his translation, " The Descent of Odin," puts it with eighteenth-century elegance :

> " Again my wearied eyes I close,
> Leave me, leave me to repose ! "

and readers of *Mansfield Park* will remember how fitly these words are applied to the languid

H

speech of Lady Bertram. A "clever fancy" on
the part of the Norns, to spin this slender thread
connecting Jane Austen (of all people!) with the
"Runick savages boozing ale!" Had she known
more of them, she would doubtless have agreed
with Frederick the Great, that all their works
were not worth a charge of powder, and that she
would have no such stuff in her library.

XIV

YOUNG SVEJDAL

1

IT was he, young Svejdal,
    Was playing at the ball;
The ball flew into the maiden's breast,
    And her cheeks grew white withal.
—Choose thy words well !

2

The ball flew into the maiden's bower,
    And after went the swain,
And or ever he left the bower behind
    She dreed full bitter pain.

3

"Oh, never shouldst thou venture
    To throw thy ball to me !
There sits a maid in a far-off land
    A-longing after thee.

4

" Oh, ne'er shalt thou seek slumber,
    And never rest shalt know,
Until thou hast loosed the lovely maid
    That long hath lain in woe ! "

5

It was he, young Svejdal,
    Wrapped him in cloak of vair,
And to the hall betook him
    To seek the captains there.

6

" Now sit in peace, my captains,
    And pledge your healths in mead,
Whiles I fare forth to the grave-mound
    To seek my mother's rede ! "

7

It was he, young Svejdal,
    That loud did cry and call,
Till the marble-stone was rent and riven
    And the mound was nigh to fall.

8

" Oh, who is it that wakes me ?
    Who calls with cry so bold ?
May I not lie and sleep in peace
    All under darksome mould ? "

9

" It is I, young Svejdal,
    Only son o' thine !
And all I ask is counsel good
    From thee, dear mother mine.

10

"My sister and my stepmother
  Have made me pale and pine,
All for a lovely lady
  That ne'er I saw with eyne."

11

"I will give thee a palfrey
  Shall serve thy need, I ween !
He can go as well o'er the salt sea-swell
  As over the land so green.

12

"A sword I will give thee also,
  Is tempered in dragon's blood,
And it will shine like a burning brand
  When thou ridest the darksome wood."

13

It was he, young Svejdal,
  That spurred his steed so free ;
Forth he rode thro' darksome wood
  And over the wide sea.

14

It was he, young Svejdal,
  That rode 'twixt sea and land ;
And he was 'ware of a herdsman there
  That drove his flock to the strand.

15

"Lithe and list, good herdsman,
  And speak thou sooth to me !
Who is it owns the flock so fair
  Thou drivest down to the sea ?"

16

"Oh, a maiden there is in this countrie
  Lies spellbound in dule and pine,
All for a swain hight Svejdal
  That never she saw with eyne."

17

"And knowest thou where the maiden dwells,
  Then hide it not from me!
Whenas I am king of all this land
  A knight I'll make of thee."

18

"Oh, yonder under the linden green
  There stands my lady's hold;
The towers are all of the marble grey,
  And the doors are decked with gold!

19

"The towers are all of the marble grey,
  And the doors are decked with gold!
Full seven years are over and gone
  Since she did sun behold.

20

"There stands a bear by my lady's bower,
  And a lion so fell to see,
But art thou Svejdal in very sooth
  Thou shalt pass by them free."

21

Forth he fared, young Svejdal,
  And up to the hold he went;
All the locks that held it
  Were riven asunder and rent.

22

The bear and the lordly lion
  They followed him from the door ;
The linden with all its silvery leaves
  Bowed down to earth before.

23

The linden bowed adown to earth
  With every silver leaf :
And up she stood, the maiden proud,
  That long had lain in grief.

24

Up she waked, the maiden proud,
  When she heard the spurs a-ringing :
" Now thanks be unto God in heaven
  Who help to me is bringing ! "

25

In he went, Sir Svejdal,
  That was both young and fair ;
It was the haughty maiden
  That hailed his entrance there.

26

" Welcome to thee, young Svejdal,
  Thou noble lord of mine !
Now praised be God in heaven
  Hath loosed us from pain and pine ! "
—Choose thy words well !

XV

THORD OF HAFSGAARD

HERE we have the Old Norse Lay of Thrym
(þrymskviða) recast and trolled forth by a mediæval minstrel.   He has been faithful to the grim
jollity of the original poem ; but, as his lilting
verse has lost the trenchant battle-axe swing of
the old alliterative metre, so the tale he tells is
shorn of the epic dignity surrounding Valhalla
and the gods.   On the restoration of the
Thunderer's hammer hangs the fate of the
Æsir in their endless warfare with the Frost
Giants ; its loss is a calamity such as was never
known in heaven nor earth.   When Freyja is
asked to play the Bride, her stamp shakes the
celestial floor.   When Thor drives to the wedding
feast, earth burns under his chariot wheels.
Whereas the Thord of the Ballad might, for
aught we are told, be a mere bonnet-laird ; and
it is only by implication that we gather any idea
of his hammer's importance.

The erudite M. Pineau (*Étude sur les Chants
Populaires Scandinaves*) is puzzled and pained
by these variations and omissions—notably that
of the Æsir's council, and of Thor's indignation
at the idea of assuming bridal attire.   " Don't

tell me," he exclaims indignantly, " that this
scene of all others could be forgotten by the
popular imagination ! " The Eddic Lays, ac-
cording to him, jealously guarded by the priests,
were never known to the people at large ; and
he goes so far as to declare that the source
alike of Lay and Ballad must be sought in some
older, and now non-existent, form of the story.
M. Pineau, in short, is a Necessitarian, who will
not allow free-will to poets. Why should not
the minstrel pick and choose his incidents ?
Why, on M. Pineau's own showing, should not
the Lay have reached him in fragmentary form ?
The student must decide for himself ; suffice it
meanwhile to say that the Ballad is a capital one,
and the " merry jest " at the end a racy substi-
tute for the ferocious pun which concludes the
original, at the expense of the Giant's mother :

> " For pence a pound was what she won."

XV

THORD OF HAFSGAARD

1

IT was Thord of Hafsgaard o'er the blowing meads did ride,
There he lost his hammer of gold, and sought for it far and
wide.

2

It was Thord of Hafsgaard spake with his brother bold :
"Thou must fare to Norrefjeld, and seek my hammer of
gold !"

3

It was little Loki that donned his feather-fell,
Forth he flew to Norrefjeld, all over the salt sea-swell.

4

All in the castle-garth his garment changèd he,
Then entered in the stone-built hall, the Giant-King to
see.

5

"Now welcome, little Loki, be thou right welcome here !
How fares the country round Hafsgaard, and the land that
lies anear ?"

6

"Well fares the country round Hafsgaard, and the land that
lies anear,
But Thord hath lost his hammer of gold, and therefore am I
come here."

7

"Never shall Thord have his hammer again, altho' ye seek
and strive !
Under the earth 'tis buried deep, full fifty fathom and five !"

8

" Never shall Thord have his hammer again (for ye shall buy
  it dear),

Till ye bring me your sister Fredensborg, with all your
  goods and gear ! "

9

It was little Loki that donned his feather-fell,

Forth he flew on the homeward way, all over the salt sea-
  swell.

10

All in the castle-garth his garment changed he,

Then entered in the stone-built hall, his brother dear to see.

11

" Never shall Thord have his hammer again, altho' we seek
  and strive,

Under the earth 'tis buried deep full fifty fathom and five !

12

" Never shall Thord have his hammer again (for we must buy
  it dear),

Till we take him our sister Fredensborg, with all our goods
  and gear ! "

13

The maiden seated on the bench she up and spake to him :

" Oh, give me to a christened man, and not to a goblin
  grim ! "

14

" Now we will take our father, and comb his locks with care,

And lead him up to Norrefjeld, all for a bride so fair ! "

15

Now true is the tale I tell ye, they took that fair young bride,

They spared no costly plenishing to deck her out with pride.

16

They seated her, that beauteous bride, upon the bridal-seat ;
Forth he came, the Giant-King, full fain the maid to greet.

17

An ox that lusty bride devoured, and thirty salted swine,
And drank, ere she could slake her thirst, twelve tuns of good
    red wine !

18

The Giant-King he paced the floor, and wrathful was his
    mood :
"Who e'er beheld a beauteous bride fall thus upon her
    food ?"

19

Up spake little Loki, beneath his cloak smiled he :
"For seven days she ate no meat, so sore she longed for
    thee ! "

20

Stayed upon a mighty tree by seven champions bold,
Up to the knees of the maiden they bore the hammer of gold.

21

Up she rose, the bride, and took the hammer in her hand ;
Good sooth, I say, she swung it light as awillow wand !

22

She slew the King o' the Giants, that Troll so fierce and
    grim,
And the lesser Trolls that sought the feast, she slew them after
    him.

23

It was little Loki that spake a merry jest :
"Our father he is a widow now, to lead him home were
    best ! "

XVI

THE AVENGING SWORD

THIS fine Ballad (admired by Andrew Lang) is unique in its mingling of pagan and Christian sentiment. The hero, who in his Bersark blood-lust spares neither wife, maid, nor suckling—whose brother the sword is possessed by a demon—who has ranged the world in pursuit of revenge—ranges it again as a penitent pilgrim, bound, for the heavier penance, in iron chains. Since, however, the Ballads concern themselves little with ecclesiastical orthodoxy, the penance is depicted as ending, not at any saintly shrine, but at the grave of his enemy.

The belief that the warrior's favourite weapons were animated by a mysterious personality is familiar to all students of Old Norse literature. One celebrated example occurs in Njàls Saga, 79, when Høgni, stealing out with Skarpheðinn by night to avenge the death of Gunnar, takes down the dead hero's halberd, and hears it singing aloud. (The O.N. impersonal idiom, "it sang in the halberd," hints at the indwelling soul.) "Then sprang up Rannveig (Gunnar's mother) and cried in bitter wrath, 'Who is taking the halberd, which I forbade all men to touch?'

'I would carry it,' said Høgni, 'to my father, that he may have it in Valhalla, and bear it at the Weapon Thing.' 'Further than that,' said she, 'wilt thou bear it, even to thy father's avenging, for the halberd declares the death of one man or more.'"

That magical forces, once unchained, might end by destroying their liberator—that the naming of the name conferred power over the name's possessor—are superstitions common to almost all primitive races.

Versions of this Ballad exist in Swedish, Norwegian, and Faroëse.

XVI
THE AVENGING SWORD

1

Sir Peter rode to the castle door,
The King of Danes he stood before.
—Forward, hurrah! ride forward.

2

"Welcome, Sir Peter, comrade mine!
Say, hast thou avenged that sire o' thine?"

3

"Oh, I ha' been so southerly
Until the sun bowed down to me.

4

"And I ha' been so westerly
Until the sun sank near to me.

5

"And I ha' been so northerly
Until the frost was frore to see.

6

"And I ha' been so easterly
Until the day was fair to see;

7

"But never did I find the wight
Could rede me my father's death aright!"

8

"Oh, say, what wilt thou give the wight
Can rede thee thy father's death aright?"

9

"Of silver he shall have his fill,
And of golden coin whate'er he will!

10

"Yea, more I'll give to him,
A ship in sailing-trim!"

11

He smiled, the King, his words to heed:
"Here stands he that did the deed!

12

"By God in heaven, I tell thee true,
None but I thy father slew!"

13

Sir Peter smote himself on the breast :
" Heart, bide still, nor break thy rest !

14

" Heart, lie still, bide patiently :
Sure and swift shall my vengeance be."

15

In the garth Sir Peter stayed
To speak with his good blade :

16

" Harken, sword so good !
Wilt drink thy fill of blood ?

17

" Good brown brand, wilt fight for me ?
No brother have I on earth but thee."

18

" Oh, say, how can I fight for thee ?
My hilt lies broken in pieces three."

19

To the smith his way he wended
That the hurt might be amended.

20

He gave him iron, he gave him steel
Of proof and price, the hurt to heal.

21

" Good brown brand, wilt fight for me ?
No brother have I on earth but thee."

22

"Be only in thy blows so stern
As I'll be swift in point to turn!

23

"Be only in thy blows so stout
As I in hilt will bear thee out!"

24

Sir Peter sought the hall
Where the knights were drinking all.

25

To prove his sword he was so fain
That seven champions straight lay slain;

26

Up and down he swung his blade,
Neither matron he spared nor maid;

27

Behind the arras there he thrust,
The King and his sons they bit the dust.

28

Up spake the babe, in cradle lay:
"A red revenge dost thou wreak to-day!

29

"A red revenge for that sire o' thine—
God give me a day for avenging mine!"

30

"And have I avenged that sire o' mine,
Shalt see no day for avenging thine!"

31

He seized the babe amain,
And struck it straight in twain.

32

"Cease, brown brand, thy thirst to slake!
Bide thou still for our Saviour's sake!"

33

Wearily whispered the sword and still:
"Fain o' thy blood I'd have my fill!

34

"Hadst thou not named my ~name, I vow
I would have slain thee, here and now!"

35

He sought the smith again,
Bade forge an iron chain.

36

He bound in chains both foot and hand,
For now would he leave for aye the land.

37

But when o'er the grave of the King he passed
The chains of iron were riven and brast.
—Forward, hurrah! ride forward.

1

XVII

THE ELFIN SHAFT

" AFTER the old gods had vanished," says Olrik, "and before the Christian God was personally apprehended, arose the rich poetry which deals with Nature-Spirits."

They always appear in the older Ballads under a grim and treacherous aspect; the Nixies, for instance, are such as we find in the " Ballad of Annan Water."

> "The bonnie grey mare did sweat with fear,
> For she heard the water-kelpie roaring."

This fear, natural to a human-kind as yet not master of the elements, was intensified by the teaching of the Church. In the Eddic mythology the Dwarfs had their own recognized place, whereas their semi-descendants, the Fairies or Nature-Spirits, not being Angels, were regarded as Devils by priestly eyes. Only in later Ballads, such as " Agnes and the Merman," and " The Mermaid's Soothsaying," do we find any hint of compassion for the soulless fay.

The theme of this Ballad—the fairy's fatal love for a mortal—originated in Northern France, whence it crept into the folk-lore of Europe in general. (Gervase of Tilbury has a warning word to young men on the dangers of elfin flirtations ; and the Rev. — Kirk in his *Secret Commonwealth* (1691) points out their "inconvenience.") The peasant of Annam, too, knows the "*con-tinh*," the wild-haired feminine Genii who dance on a starless night, and lure mortal youths to their undoing.

To the Elfin Shaft or Elfin Bolt was attributed sudden death or seizure of pain, either in man or beast, among the Scandinavians.

The Icelandic form of the Ballad heightens the horror by the addition of those fiery portents associated with burial-houses containing treasure, guarded by fairies or by the dead. The "false fairy" stabs Sir Oluf with a sword, which, under cover of her cloak, she takes from her "treasure chest of gold."

> "Sign ye your brows with the holy cross,
>   (They will woo him to undo him)
> Sancta Maria, watch over us !
>   (See the red flames leaping high !
> Blithe lay the bower beneath the fells,
> Blithe lay the bower the fells hard by.) "

XVII

THE ELFIN SHAFT

1

Sir Oluf hath ridden west and east
To bid his friends to his bridal feast.
—Gay goes the dance by the greenwood tree.

2

By the howe he took his way,
And there danced elf and fay.

3

There they danced in blithesome band ;
The Elf-king's daughter reached forth her hand.

4

The Elf-king's daughter her hand stretched she :
" And will Sir Oluf tread a measure with me ? "

5

" I may not, I dare not, the measure tread !
To-morrow morn shall I be wed."

6

" Oh, tread now a measure, Sir Oluf, with me !
Two buckskin boots will I give to thee,

7

" Boots well beseeming a knight so bold,
With spurs thereto of red, red gold.

8

"Oh, tread now a measure, Sir Oluf, with me!
A silken kirtle I'll give to thee,

9

"A silken kirtle so fair and fine
That my mother bleached in the pale moonshine."

10

"I may not, I dare not, the measure tread!
To-morrow morn shall I be wed."

11

"Oh, tread now a measure, Sir Oluf, with me!
An orb of gold I will give to thee."

12

"An orb of gold I fain would win,
But I may not dance with the fairy kin."

13

"And if thou wilt not dance with me,
Scathe and sickness shall follow thee!"

14

She struck Sir Oluf under his heart,
Deep in its roots he felt the smart.

15

She lifted him up on his horse of pride:
"Go home, go home, and seek thy bride!"

16

Oh, he rode up to his castle door,
And it was his mother that stood before.

17

"Lithe now and listen, Sir Oluf my son,
Why is thy cheek so white and wan?"

18

"Well may my cheek be wan and white,
I have seen the elf-maids' sport to-night!"

19

"Lithe now and listen, dear son of mine,
What shall I say to that bride of thine?"

20

"Shalt say I am in the mead
A-proving hound and steed."

21

All on the morrow ere dawn was grey
The bride rode in with glad array

22

They poured the mead and they poured the wine:
"Now where is Sir Oluf, dear bridegroom mine?"

23

"Sir Oluf is in the mead
A-proving hound and steed."

24

"Oh, doth he love hound and horse of pride
Better than he loves his bride?"

25

She sought him alow, she sought him aloft,
She found Sir Oluf sleeping soft.

26

She lifted the cloak of scarlet red,
There lay Sir Oluf, was cold and dead.

27

She kissed him in the bridal-bower,
She died herself the self-same hour.

28

All so early, ere dawn was red,
Were three in Sir Oluf's hold lay dead.

29

Sir Oluf lay dead, and his bride alsò;
The third was his mother, that died for woe.
—The dance goes gay by the greenwood tree.

XVIII, XIX
THE KNAVISH MERMAN
AGNES AND THE MERMAN

THAT the first of these Ballads is the more
ancient appears probable through its conception
of the Merman—the grim troll with his shape-
changing and his glamour, fit image of the in-
exorable sea. The fine imaginative touch of the
holy images averting their heads must have been
borrowed from this by the later Ballad. Versions

exist in Swedish, Norwegian, Faroëse, Icelandic, and English ("Clerk Colvill and the Mermaid ").

The "Agnes" Ballad must, I take it, have been known to Matthew Arnold, who enriched its simple folk-melody with the elaborate orchestration of his "Forsaken Merman." But, for dramatic power and genuine feeling, the honours remain with the more primitive bard.

It dates from the late mediæval period when creative power was on the wane, and is an adaptation of the German "Schöne Agnete"—which, in its turn, has a Slav original. The German Ballad, however, takes the more primitive view of the Merman, who ends by destroying his mortal mistress. Later Danish minstrels—Sven Grundtvig among them—have altered the conclusion accordingly.

XVIII

THE KNAVISH MERMAN

I

Gay goes the dance in the kirkyard there,
  —Welladay—
They dance, the knights, with blades so bare,
  —Methinks 'tis hard to ride away.

2

They dance, the maidens, with hair unbound ;
It was the King's daughter sang the round.

3

Proud was the Princess, sweet was her song ;
That heard the Merman, the waves among.

4

Up rose the Merman, thus spake he :
" Perchance the King's daughter will wed with me ! "

5

Garments he shaped and a golden ring,
He called him Sir Alfast, son of a King.

6

He shaped him a steed so black and bold,
He rode like a knight in a saddle of gold.

7

He tied his steed where the shade was mirk,
Withershins went he round the kirk.

8

Into the kirk the Merman hied,
And all the holy images they turned their heads aside

9

Up spake the priest by the altar that stood :
"Who may he be, this knight so good ? "

10

The Princess smiled, her cloak behind :
" Now would to God the knight were mine ! "

11

"Listen, proud Princess, and love thou me!
A crown of gold I'll give to thee."

12

"Over three kingdoms my father was King,
But ne'er did he give me so fair a thing."

13

He wrapped her in his cloak of blue,
Forth from the kirk they fared, they two.

14

They met all on the wold
The steed with saddle of gold.

15

As they rode o'er the lea
He became a troll, so foul to see.

16

When they rode down to the water's brim
He became a troll, so fierce and grim.

17

"Sir Alfast, thou art christened man,
What wilt thou with this water wan?"

18

"No knight am I, nor christened man,
My dwelling is in this water wan!"

19

And when they reached the midmost Sound
Fifty fathom they sank to ground.

20

Long heard the fishers with dread and dree
How the King's daughter sobbed under the sea!
—Welladay!
Methinks 'tis hard to ride away.

XIX

AGNES AND THE MERMAN

1

AGNES she walked on the edge of the steep,
And up came a Merman out from the deep.
—Ha ha ha!
Up came a Merman out from the deep.

2

"Lithe now and listen, Agnes, to me,
And say if thou wilt my true-love be?"

3

"Yes, good sooth, that will I be
Wilt thou bear me down to the depths o' the sea."

4

Oh, he has stopped her ears and stopped her mouth
    beside,
And borne her down all under the tide.

5

There she dwelt eight years and more,
Seven sons she to the Merman bore.

6

Agnes she sat by the cradle and sang,
And she heard how the bells of England rang.

7

She to the Merman did speak and say:
"May I go up in the kirk to pray?"

8

"Thou hast my leave to go withal,
But see thou come back to thy children small.

9

"When to the kirkyard thou dost fare,
Then see thou let not down thy shining golden hair.

10

"And when thou enterest in the door
Then sit by thy mother's side no more.

11

"When the priest names the Name of dread,
Then bow not down thy head."

12

Oh, he has stopped her ears and stopped her mouth
    amain,
And so he bore her up to England's shores again.

13

When thro' the kirkyard she did fare,
Oh then did she let down her shining golden hair.

14

And when she entered in the door
She sat by her mother, as of yore.

15

When the priest named the Name of dread,
Then she bowed down her head.

16

"Agnes, my daughter, I ask of thee,
Where hast thou been eight years away from me?"

17

"I dwelt in the sea eight years and more,
Seven sons I to the Merman bore."

18

"Now tell me, daughter, and fear no blame,
What did he give for thy maiden fame?"

19

"He gave me a ring of golden sheen,
Never a better one hath the Queen.

20

"Of golden shoon he gave me a pair,
Never a better the Queen might wear.

21

"He gave me a harp of gold to play
That I might touch its strings and wile my cares
away."

22

The Merman he made him a path so strait
Up from the strand to the kirkyard gate.

23

Into the kirk the Merman hied,
And all the holy images they turned their heads aside.

24

Like the purest gold was his shining hair,
His eyes were full of sorrow and care.

25

" Lithe now and listen, Agnes, to me ;
All thy little children are longing after thee!"

26

" Let them long as they will, let their longing be sore,
I shall return to them nevermore!"

27

"Oh, think of the big ones and think of the small!
Of the baby in the cradle think thou most of all."

28

"I think not of the big ones, I think not of the small,
Of the baby in the cradle I'll think least of all!"
—Ha ha ha!
Of the baby in the cradle I'll think least of all.

XX
THE ENCHANTED MAIDEN

THE story told by this Ballad takes us into no very remote region of Faërie ; wicked stepdame, enchanted maid, and knightly deliverer are all familiar personages. The belief in human blood as means whereby the bewitched mortal is delivered from the beast-likeness is found in the folk-lore of many nations, and may be a dim memory of sacrificial cannibal feasts. But the beautiful Introductory Stanzas are noteworthy ; for such detailed descriptions of Nature occur but rarely in Ballads, Danish or other. This one recalls the famous opening of one among the Ballads of Robin Hood :

> "In summer when the shawes be sheen,
>   And leves be large and long,
> It is full merrie in fair forest
>   To hear the foulës' song,
>
> "To see the deere draw to the dale,
>   And leave the hillës hie,
> And shelter them in the levës greene,
>   Under the greenwood tree."

A verse of another Danish Ballad might have been spoken by Little John, who bids his " dere

master " pluck up heart, " and think this is a
merrie time, all in a morning of May " :

> " Os fry der Aarsens Tid og Tag
>   det Maj i Morgen er ;
> den kommer os alle til Behag
>   alt baade tjern og nær."

XX

THE ENCHANTED MAIDEN

Oʜ, well I wot where the greenwood grows
  That standeth beside the firth,
And in it there grow the fairest trees
  That a man may see on earth !

Therein the willow and linden grow,
  The fairest a man may find,
And under them play the lordly beasts
  That men call hart and hind.

There they play, both hind and hart,
  And the beasts of the fair forest,
And there she plays, the lily-white hind,
  With gold beneath her breast.

1

It was Nilus Erlandsson
  Rode forth the deer to take ;
There he saw the lily-white hind
  'That ran thro' bush and brake.
—So the knight hath won his lady.

2

After went Nilus Erlandsson
  That longed for her so sore ;
But never might he reach the hind
  For three days' space and more.

3

Snares he set on every path
  Where'er the hind might go,
But all so cunning was she
  He might not take her so.

4

Sir Nilus thro' the greenwood
  Rode after her in vain ;
His hounds he loosed by two, by three,
  To run her down amain.

5

So hot the hounds went on her trail
  That never might she 'scape ;
She changed her all by grammarye
  And fled in a falcon's shape.

6

She shaped her as a falcon fleet,
  And perched in the linden green ;
Under the tree Sir Nilus stood
  And sighed for toil and tene.

7

Sir Nilus took an axe in hand
  To fell the linden-tree,
When out there sprang a yeoman fierce
  That smote the shaft in three.

K

8

"And wilt thou fell my father's wood
  And all by wrongful power,
I swear to thee, Nilus Erlandsson,
  Thou shalt abye it sore!"

9

"Now let me fell this single tree,
  This tree alone of thine,
For, but I take the falcon fair,
  I die of dule and pine!"

10

"Now lithe and listen, thou fair young knight,
  To the counsel that I bring;
Ne'er shalt thou take her until she taste
  The flesh of a tamèd thing!"

11

A gobbet he hewed from out his breast,
  (And that was mickle pain!)
She spread her wings and down she flew
  And fell on the bait amain.

12

She spread her wings and down she flew
  And on the bait she fell;
She changed her shape to the fairest maid
  That ever tongue might tell.

13

She stood in a sark of silk so red
  Where the linden-tree did blow;
The knight he took her in his arms,
  And there she wept her woe.

14

"Oh, I sat and broidered lily and rose,
   I guided my father's gear,
When in she came, my false stepdame,
   That never held me dear.

15

" She shaped me all as a lily-white hind
   To run in fair greenwood,
And myseven maidens as seven wolves,
   And bade them have my blood."

16

The maid stood under the linden-tree,
   And loosed her golden hair,
And thither they came that erst were wolves,
   Her seven maidens fair.

17

" Now thanks to thee, Nilus Erlandsson,
   Hast loosed me from sore alarms !
Never shalt thou seek slumber
   But in my lily-white arms.

18

"Now thanks to thee, Nilus Erlandsson,
   Hast saved me from pain and pest !
Never shalt thou seek slumber
   But on my lily-white breast."
—So the knight hath won his lady.

MISCELLANEOUS BALLADS

XXI, XXII

TORBEN'S DAUGHTER
THE MAIDEN AT THE THING

"Torben's Daughter" is a fine example of compressed, dramatic narration—we are not even told the names of hero and heroine. It is interesting also as depicting the simplicity of antique manners, when a knight might be found holding the plough. The maiden who pledges her father's slayer, behaves, though in all innocence, as does the false wife of the Baron of Brackley:

"The lady she feasted them, carried them ben,
  She laughed wi' the men that her baron had slain."

The second Ballad is that which, greatly daring, sings the praises of simple worth—thus expressing a tendency doomed by the spirit of later times. Unlike the reprover of Clara Vere de Vere, the minstrel adorns his theme with a dry humour, that spares neither hero nor heroine—dowdy country maid and dandified lordling. That is an excellent touch (verse 3) which shows the former's resentment of the pert page's remarks on her garments ; so is her artful reference to the excellent appetite which will reward her future lord's agricultural exertions—the ancient wisdom of "Feed the brute!" The Ballad craves a sequel, to be entitled "The Husband turned Husbandman."

XXI

TORBEN'S DAUGHTER

OH, we were many sisters small,
  —On the lea—
So early did our father fall.
—The day it is dawning, and the dew it is falling so free.

I

All on a Sunday evening they scoured both spear and
    sword,
All on a Monday morning wrathful they rode abroad.

2

When they went by the northern shaw
Sir Torben ploughing his land they saw.

3

"There standst thou, Sir Torben, so fair and fine !
Now pay me blood-money for kinsman mine."

4

"I will give thee farm and stead,
I will give thee my daughter, so fair a maid."

5

"We come not hither for house nor land,
We come for the blood of thy red right hand!'

6

They hewed Sir Torben to pieces small
As the leaves that under the linden fall.

7

They're ridden up to Sir Torben's stead,
And there stood his daughter, so fair a maid.

8

She stood, as slim as a willow-wand,
With a goblet of gold in either hand.

9

She poured the wine with sport and play,
She pledged the man who her sire did slay.

10

"Now had I guessed thee so mild of mood,
I ne'er had spilt thy father's blood!"

11

"And if thou hast my father slain,
Then I must dree right bitter pain."

12

"And have I done ill to thee thereby
Thou shalt fare hereafter as well as I."

13

He set her up on his steed so true,
He wrapped her in his cloak of blue.

14

They rode away o'er the darksome heather,
—On the lea—
Never more did she see her father.
—The day it is dawning, and the dew it is falling so free.

XXII

THE MAIDEN AT THE THING

1

Young was Inge the maid,
—In the green grove—
Yet she rode to the Thing unafraid.
—To ride to the maiden's bower.

2

Up and spake to his knights the King:
"I spy a maiden that rides to the Thing!"

3

The little foot-page he answered then:
"Oh, she comes here a-riding to gaze upon the men!

4

"But see her kirtle's old-fashioned shape,
And only look on her ill-cut cape!"

5

For all the maiden was so meek
She heard each word the page did speak.

6

"And if my heart had felt no tene,
I had been better at home, I ween!

7

" And did I not know mine errand well,
I had been better at home to dwell!

8

" But my kirtle hath no ill-favoured shape,
And after the mode is cut my cape.

9

" Thou King o' Danes, now hark and hear;
A plaint have I for thy gracious ear.

10

" I was but a little child
Whenas I lost my mother mild.

11

" My father set me on his knee,
And divided with me both gold and fee.

12

" But he died or ever two years were done;
O'er house and lands I must rule alone.

13

" But in there came my uncles three,
All my goods they waste from me.

14

" The mown they mar, the sown they spoil,
Both man and maid they lure from toil.

15

" Oxen and kine they drive abroad,
They wile my serving-men from my board.

16

" Ere I'll live longer without relief
I'll give thee my father's lands in fief ! "

17

" Now thanks to thee for thy gift, O maid !
Say, which of my knights thou fain wouldst wed ? "

18

" And may I speak as my choice is made,
'Tis Sir Ove Stison I fain would wed."

19

" Stand up, Sir Ove, and answer free ;
Here is a maiden will marry thee ! "

20

Up stood Sir Ove, and answered so free :
" Fair maiden, nought shalt thou win from me !

21

" Better can I tie a silken band
Than play the farmer on lea and land.

22

" Better can I ride with hawk and hound
Than drive the plough through the heavy ground ! "

23

" Oh, sit in my chariot all by me,
So good a farmer I'll make of thee !

24

" Take plough in hand, lay the furrow featly,
Take corn in hand, and scatter it meetly.

25

"And let the harrow after go,
Thou'lt make a goodly farmer so;

26

"And of thy meat thou'lt be so fain
That men will call thee a right true Dane!"

27

To laugh and be merry men were not loth
When Sir Ove plighted the maid his troth.

28

All alone to the Thing she hied,
The King he led her home again, and all his swains beside.
—In the green grove,
To ride to the maiden's bower.

XXIII, XXIV

THE GAME OF DICE
KING ERIK AND THE SCORNFUL
MAID

THESE two Ballads deal, from different stand-
points, with the change of manners that came in
towards the close of the Middle Ages. A barrier
grew up between bower and hall; the Squire
became the serving man, whose menial labours
were no longer shared by his master. There

were those, doubtless, who regretted the good old times ; and the " King Erik " Ballad expresses their sentiments.

"The Game of Dice," with its more conventional ending, is concerned for gentility. Its Danish version dates from the twelfth or thirteenth century. Other forms exist in Norwegian and Icelandic, and in a Swedish broadsheet of the later eighteenth century. There is also a Slav version.

XXIII

THE GAME OF DICE

1

"Harken here, thou good young swain,
  And play at dice with me !"
"Oh, ne'er have I the ruddy gold
  To wager here with thee."
—Because they played, and threw the dice of gold.

2

"Oh, wager now thy goodly hat,
  Altho' it be of grey,
And I will wager my snood of pearl,
  Shalt take it, an thou may !"

3

When first the dice of gold
　Upon the board did run,
The youth he lost his wager,
　And glad the maiden won.

4

"Harken here, thou good young swain,
　And cast the dice with me!"
"Oh, ne'er have I the ruddy gold
　To wager here with thee."

5

"Now wager thou thy kirtle,
　Altho' it be of grey,
And I will wager my golden crown,
　Shalt take it, an thou may!"

6

When next the dice of gold
　Upon the board did run,
The youth he lost his wager,
　And glad the maiden won.

7

"Harken here, thou good young swain,
　And play at dice with me!"
"Oh, ne'er have I the ruddy gold
　To wager here with thee."

8

"Thy hosen shalt thou wager,
　And shoon shalt wager both;
I'll set thereto my honour,
　But and my plighted troth."

9

And when the dice of gold
  Upon the board were cast,
The youth he won the wager,
  And sad the maiden lost.

10

" Harken here, young jackanapes,
  And get thee gone from me !
My knife adorned with silver
  That will I give to thee."

11

"Thy knife adorned with silver
  I'll take it when I may ;
But I will have the maiden
  I won with dice at play ! "

12

" Harken here, young jackanapes,
  And get thee gone from me !
Seven silk-sewn kirtles
  All will I give to thee."

13

" Thy seven silk-sewn kirtles
  I'll take whenas I may ;
But I will have the maiden
  I won with dice at play ! "

14

" Harken here, young jackanapes,
  And get thee gone from me !
A white steed and saddle
  Those will I give to thee."

15

"White steed and saddle
  I'll take whene'er I may ;
But I will have the maiden
  I won with dice at play ! "

16

"Harken here, young jackanapes,
  And get thee gone from me !
My hold and my castle
  Those will I give to thee."

17

"Thy hold and thy castle
  I'll take them when I may ;
But I will have the maiden
  I won with dice at play ! "

18

The maiden sought her bower,
  And there her locks arrayed :
"Now for the match that I must make
  God help me, luckless maid ! "

19

All with his sword a-playing
  The youth he up and spake :
"Oh, better far than thy deserts
  The match that thou shalt make !

20

"For I am ne'er a jackanapes,
  Altho' it be thy word ;
I am the noblest son of kings
  That ever walked abroad ! "

21

"Art thou the noblest son of kings
    That ever walked abroad,
Then shalt thou have mine honour,
    But and my plighted word!"
—Because they played, and threw the dice of gold.

XXIV

KING ERIK AND THE SCORNFUL MAID

1

ALL so rich a damsel
    Dwells southward in our land,
And ne'er to dance with a poor young swain
    Will she stretch forth her hand.
—Damsel, great is thy favour! I thank thee right
    courteously.

2

Ne'er to dance with a poor young swain
    Will she hold forth her hand;
She's tied up her sleeves with ribbons of silk
    And many a golden band.

3

It was young King Erik
    Bade saddle his steed so free:
"Forth will we fare to the southland
    And visit this proud ladye!"

4

It was young King Erik
  That forth to dance did stand ;
He's taken that dainty damsel
  All by her lily hand.

5

"Now nay, I will not dance with thee !
  Too hard are thy hands indeed ;
Thou hast been hewing of hedges
  Or spreading of muck on the mead !"

6

"Oh, yestre'en I played at a bridal-feast,
  A-tilting with knights so tall,
And hard is my hand with grasping the brand
  That won me the prize from all !"

7

"And wert thou yestre'en at a bridal-feast
  There tilted no knights so tall !
Wert loading thy father's wain with muck,
  And deeper in dirt than all.

8

"Ill they become thee, thy garments,
  Thy hosen are rent at the knee ;
Thy master hath given thee holiday,
  So thou must ride speedilie !"

9

"Are there no tailors, women or men,
  Here in this town o' thine,
Can cut me clothes of the scarlet cloth
  And sew them with silk so fine ?"

10

"Tailors there are, both women and men,
    Here in this town o' mine,
Can cut thee breeches of wadmal coarse
    And sew them with hempen twine."

11

"Lithe and listen, thou haughty maid,
    Wilt yield thy love to me?
All the gold that in Denmark lies
    Thy portion it shall be!"

12

"All the gold that in Denmark lies
    Is held in strong duresse;
Get thee gone and patch thy shoon!
    Thy feet will ache the less."

13

Up spake the lady's serving-maid
    As boldly as she might:
"And it is young King Erik
    That thou dost scorn and spite!"

14

"And is it young King Erik
    That I have scorned and shent,
Methinks I ha' done an evil deed,
    And sore do I repent.

15

"All in the midst o' my father's garth
    There standeth a linden green,
And many a knight and lady fair
    Hold tryst beneath unseen!"

L

16

"All in the midst o' thy father's garth
There standeth a linden green,
And many a thief and rascal wight
Hold tryst beneath unseen!"
—Lady, great is thy favour! I thank thee right courteously.

XXV

THE MAIDEN'S MORNING DREAM

THIS Ballad is a special favourite throughout Scandinavia. S. Grundtvig dates it from the twelfth century, the period of the Wendish invasions, and inclines to consider it as founded on fact. But, as Olrik points out, the Wend King here rides up, not as marauder, but as fairy prince; so that the Ballad was probably composed later, and borrowed his figure—a shadow of "old, unhappy, far-off things"—from earlier ones composed during the time of Wendish warfare. My translation of verse 21 hardly does justice to the original :

"Vesselil ind at Døren tren,
    da var det ret som Solen sken."

XXV

THE MAIDEN'S MORNING DREAM

1

To the bower went Riseli,
(But a Frankish mile away)
And the maid awakened she.
(The Wends come up to the castle.)

2

With honour and praise should maidens awake,
But a whip for the waking did Riseli take.

3

"If thou dost lie and sleep so late,
Never a knight wilt thou win for mate!"

4

"Oh, better I love my morning dream
Than other maids their silken seam!

5

"Methought I was but a spirit light,
To the land o' the Wends I took my flight.

6

"So wide my wings were spanned
They covered lea and land.

7

"I set me down on a linden-root,
And the branches bowed beneath my foot."

8

"Now heed, O niece, what I say to thee;
Shalt give thy morning dream to me!

9

"Shalt give to me thy morning dream,
And I'll give thee all my summer's seam."

10

"Oh, keep thyself thy summer's seam!
Far dearer to me is my morning dream."

11

Oh, scarcely had they done debate,
When the Wendish King rode up to the gate.

12

The Wendish King rode up to the door,
Riseli went and stood before.

13

"Welcome, noble lord of mine!
Now shall I pour thee mead or wine?"

14

"I will have nor mead nor wine,
But I will see Vesselil, niece o' thine!"

15

"But five years old is Vesselil,
She bides with her foster-mother still."

16

"And an she were but three years old,
These eyes the maiden must behold!"

17

"My other maids sit sewing still,
But never of sleep can she have her fill."

18

Into the hall the King she led,
And forth to seek her niece she sped.

19

Her hair she tore, her face she struck:
"Woe worth thee, Vesselil, for thy good luck!

20

"Now do thou on thy garments bright,
For thou shalt see the King to-night."

21

Into the hall did Vesselil fare,
And it seemed as the sun shone in with her.

22

"Oh, never a maiden did I behold
Was grown so well for five years old!"

23

He stroked her on her cheek so white,
He called her love and heart's delight.

24

"I give thee my word, O Vesselil,
Shalt sleep as long as thou hast a will."

25

They clad her all in silken weed,
They lifted her on the good grey steed.

26

They set on her head a crown of gold,
And the King he led her from the hold
—But a Frankish mile away—
The Wends come up to the castle.

XXVI

SIR KAREL'S LYKE-WAKE

THIS sixteenth-century Ballad has a Scots parallel
in " Willie's Wake," and versions of the same
story are found in Italy, Hungary, Bulgaria, and
Galicia ; but whether it travelled from south to
north, or vice versa, cannot be determined.　Little
Kirsten's self-betrayal in owning her love for the
supposedly dead man is peculiar to the Northern
form.　The wistful, delicate humour, moreover,
of the two concluding verses, seems to me charac-
teristically Danish—their author, a literary ancestor
of Hans Andersen.

I

IT was young Sir Karel
　His mother's rede did pray,
If he snou.d to the cloister ride
　And bear his love away.
—The roses and the lilies all a-blowing.

2

"Shalt seem to die, a corse shalt lie
   In shroud the bier upon,
And ne'er a one will seek to prove
   If thou art living man."

3

Late, so late at even
   The sickness on him fell;
All in the morning early
   They tolled for him the bell.

4

They've ta'en him, young Sir Karel,
   And streeked him for a corse,
And all to tell the tidings
   His page has taken horse.

5

Up and into the cloister
   All with the bier they hied,
The Prior came to meet them
   With mickle pomp and pride.

6

Forth they went, the singing-boys,
   Clad all in scarlet red,
They bade the maidens come to watch:
   "For young Sir Karl is dead.

7

It was little Kirsten
   Spake with her mother dear:
"And may I to the watching wend
   Over Sir Karel's bier?"

8

"Yea, do thou on thy scarlet weed,
　　And deck thy head with gold;
But be thou 'ware of young Sir Karl,
　　His wiles are manifold!"

9

She entered in, the little maid,
　　Amid the tapers' shine,
She could not see them burning bright,
　　So tearful were her eyne.

10

Beside his head she sat her down,
　　And for his soul she prayed:
"Alas, thou wast my heart's delight
　　In the days ere thou wast dead!"

11

Beside his feet she sat her down,
　　And smoothed the linen white:
"Oh, in the days ere thou wast dead
　　Thou wast my heart's delight!"

12

Right softly then he up and spake:
　　"Now cease from tene and tear,
For lo, 'tis all for love of thee
　　I lie upon the bier!

13

"My steed stands in the cloister garth
　　A-tarrying all for thee;
Wilt thou now, little Kirsten,
　　Fare forth afar with me!"

14

It was young Sir Karel
  Rose straightway from the dead;
And as they reached the cloister door
  A gay good-night she bade.

15

The nuns they all sat silent,
  And on their books read they,
They thought 'twas GOD's good angel
  That bore the maid away.

16

The nuns they all sat silent,
  Each to herself said she:
"GOD grant that His good angel
  May come eftsoon for me!"
—The roses and the lilies all a-blowing.

XXVII

AAGE AND ELSE

THIS Ballad may be compared with our own
"Sweet William and May Margaret," "Sweet
William's Ghost," and the conclusion of "Clerk
Saunders." The same theme gave rise to Ballads
in Sweden, Brittany, Germany, Spain, Italy,
Greece, and the Slav countries. (The idea of
a dead lover's return to his sweetheart is one so

natural that we surely need not hark back for its Danish source to the classical Lay of Helge and Sigrun.) It inspires another fine Ballad, "Sir Morten of Fuglsang," whose Burden was borrowed by Longfellow in his poetical version of Olaf Tryggvason's Saga (*Tales of a Wayside Inn*).

The line in verse 6, "*No cloak had he*," refers to the custom of smiting the door with a fold of the cloak. (In "Niels Ebbeson" I have substituted "sword," as more intelligible to the English reader.)

The metre of "Aage and Else" is an interesting variation on the usual form of the four-lined stanza.

XXVII

AAGE AND ELSE

1

THREE maidens sat in a bower,
  Two broidered with gold
The third she wept her own true love
  All under darksome mould.
(For she loved the knight so truly.)

2

It was the Knight Sir Aage
  Went riding here and there,
He loved the lady Elselil,
  A maid so fair.

3

He wooed the lady Elselil
  With gifts and gold ;
On Monday thereafter
  He lay in the mould.

4

Sore wept she, lady Elselil,
  With wellaway ;
That heard the knight Sir Aage
  Low where he lay.

5

Up stood the knight Sir Aage,
  His coffin took amain,
Forth to his true love's bower he fared
  With mickle pain.

6

He knocked there with his coffin—
  No cloak had he—
"Stand up, thou stately Elselil,
  Open to me!"

7

Up spake the lady Elselil,
  With tears spake she :
"Canst thou name the name of Jesu
  I'll open to thee!"

8

"Stand up, thou lady Elselil,
  Open thy door !
I can name the name of Jesu
  As ever I could of yore."

9

Up stood she, stately Elselil,
  With drearihed ;
There opened she her bower door,
  Let in the dead.

10

She took her golden comb
  To smooth his hair ;
For every lock she ordered
  Down fell a tear.

11

"Lithe and listen, Sir Aage,
  Dearest love mine,
How goes it under darksome earth
  In grave o' thine ?"

12

"So goes it under the darksome earth
  Where I am laid
As in the happy realm of heaven ;
  Therefore be glad."

13

"Lithe and listen, Sir Aage,
  Dearest love mine.
Fain would I lie 'neath darksome mould
  All in that grave o' thine."

14

"So is it under darksome mould,
  There where I rest,
As in the blackest depths of hell
  —Cross thou thy breast

15

" For every tear thou sheddest
    In mournful mood,
Down into my grave doth fall
    A drop of blood.

16

" Up above my head
    The green grass grows ;
Round about my feet
    The wild worm goes.

17

" Now in the darksome entry
    The black cock doth crow,
And all the gates are opening ;
    Forth must I go.

18

" Now crows upon the high-loft
    The cock so red,
And I must go to the kirkyard
    With all the dead."

19

Up stood the knight Sir Aage,
    His coffin took again,
Forth fared he to the kirkyard
    With mickle pain.

20

Up stood she, stately Elselil,
    Right mournful was her mood ;
She followed him, her own true love,
    Through the wild wood.

21

As thro' the wood they wended
  All to the kirkyard there,
Wan it grew and faded,
  His goodly golden hair.

22

" Behold now up in heaven
  The stars so bright ;
So shalt thou see soothly
  How goes the night."

23

She saw them up in heaven,
  The stars so fair ;
Down in the earth the dead man sank
  Ere she was ware.

24

Home went she, lady Elselil,
  With care so cold ;
On Monday thereafter
  Lay she in the mould.
(For she loved the knight so truly.)

XXVIII, XXIX
LOVEL AND JOHN
TYGE HERMANDSSON

Jovial Ballads, these, of the Young Lochinvar type, where the too tardy bridegroom wins the verdict "Serve him right!" (In the former, I have made free with the name of Sir Lave, turning it into Lovel.) The *svalegang* plays its part in the story, since it is along this open gallery-stair that Sir John lights the bride to her bower. The Burden is handled with singular skill; the concluding line in verses 2, 3, and 4 forms no part of the dialogue, but is an aside spoken by the poet.

"Gallant knight" in "Tyge Hermandsson," v. 21, is literally "lady's swain" (Jomfrusvend) —squire of dames, first in love as in war.

XXVIII
LOVEL AND JOHN

Lo now, I bid you, my merry men all,
    Put your armour on! [1]
Bind on your helms of the burning gold,
    And follow Sir John!

---

[1] Lit : Be ye well boun ! (I være vel bon.)

1

Sir Peter home from the Thing did fare,
  (Put your armour on)
Forth came little Kirsten to meet him there,
  And ask after John.

2

" Welcome, dear father, home from the Thing!
  (Put your armour on)
Tell me what tidings hast thou to bring ? "
  What news of Sir John ?

3

" These are the tidings I have for thee,
  (Put your armour on)
That young Sir Lovel thy bridegroom shall be."
  And not Sir John.

4

" If young Sir Lovel my bridegroom shall be,
  (Put your armour on)
Sorrow and care shall he have with me ! "
  While he lives, Sir John.

5

Sir Lovel to bridal-feast doth speed,
  (Put your armour on)
Sir John hath bidden them shoe his steed.
  " I go with him," said John.

6

Sir John he rode to the blithe bridàle,
  (Put your armour on)
High on his horse in his coat of mail.
  " I come ! " said John.

7

When the dew fell fast and the eve was sped,
  (Put your armour on)
The bride must go to the bridal-bed.
  "I go thither!" said John.

8

They led the bride to the bridal-bower,
  (Put your armour on)
Sir John he carried the torch before.
  "I first," said John.

9

Sir John he locked the door aright:
  (Put your armour on)
"Now bid Sir Lovel a gay good-night!"
  All from Sir John.

10

Straight to Sir Lovel the news they cried:
  (Put your armour on)
"Sir John he sleeps with thy fair young bride!"
  That did Sir John.

11

Now when the day was dawning there
  (Put your armour on)
Sir Lovel forth to the king did fare.
  "I go with him!" said John.

12

"My gracious lord, now hark and heed!
  (Put your armour on)
A plaint have I that craves for rede."
  "'Tis of me," said John.

M

13

"A fair young bride I thought to wed,
  (Put your armour on)
But another knight took the bride instead!"
  "That was I," said John.

14

"And if ye both hold the maid so dear,
  (Put your armour on)
Now for her sake ye shall break a spear "
  "I shall win!" said John.

15

The first of the courses they rode so free,
  (Put your armour on)
Sir Lovel's horse fell on his knee.
  "Hold up!" said John.

16

And when they rode to the joust again,
  (Put your armour on)
Sir Lovel's neck was broken in twain.
  "Lie there!" said John.

17

She clapped her hands, the dainty dame :
  (Put your armour on)
"Ne'er did I see so fair a game!"
  Thus he won, Sir John.
—Bind on your helmets of burning gold,
  And follow Sir John!

XXIX

TYGE HERMANDSSON

1

ALL on a Saturday morning it rained both far and wide,
And it was Tyge Hermandsson that should fetch home his
bride.
—I will ride forth to seek for a fair one.

2

The knight looked forth from the window, the burn it ran so
high :
"My bride is not so dear to me that I for her should die!

3

" Now harken, Nilaus Bendiktsson, long-leggèd is thy steed !
Fetch home my bride for love of GOD, and help me in my
need ! "

4

Up spake Nilaus Bendiktsson, he spake a word so free :
" And if I fetch thee home thy bride, be sure I'll cozen thee ! "

5

It was Nilaus Bendiktsson that rode the bride to meet,
Silk and samite floated about his horse's feet.

6

His swains were clothed in samite, with owches of gold beside ;
Unto the kirk they've ridden, all with the fair young bride.

7

The bride she stood at kirkyard gate, red as a rose in bloom ;
She looked out over the water : " And where is the bonny
groom ? "

8

Up spake Nilaus Bendiktsson, he spake right joyfully :
" He dared not cross the burn to-day, for the water ran so
high ! "

9

All on the bridal-bench the bride right modestly she sate,
They looked out over the water : " The bridegroom tarries
late ! "

10

They poured in cups of silver the mead and wine so red ;
All in the evening early the bride must seek her bed.

11

They led her in, the fair young bride, all to her chamber door,
Forth went knights and pages to bear the torch before.

12

Oh, they laid her in the bridal-bed, and she was a dainty dame.
She tarried there three hours and more, and ne'er a bridegroom came.

13

The priests they stood by the bridal-bed, and sang as best
they mote ;
" Now who shall sleep beside our bride, since the bridegroom
cometh not ? "

14

Up stood Nilaus Bendiktsson, cast off his silver shoon :
" Now I will plight her faith and troth and sleep by her
eftsoon ! "

15

I wot their hearts were merry as they pledged the bonny
    bride,
All save Tyge Hermandsson, dared not the water ride.

16

Now on the Wednesday after the flood began to fall;
Over came Tyge Hermandsson, but and his followers all.

17

It was Tyge Hermandsson did to the castle fare,
She stood without, the bonny bride, wrapped all in cloak of
    vair.

18

Oh, high she held her head, I wis, and spake with haughty
    cheer :
" Away with thee, Tyge Hermandsson, no welcome hast thou
    here ! "

19

" Now lithe and listen, proud Liselil, this blame I have for
    thee,
Hast plighted troth with another man, so hast thou cozened
    me ! "

20

" Harken, Tyge Hermandsson, this word I tell thee plain,
Never, ah, never I'll wed the man dares not ride out in the
    rain !

" Now hadst thou been a gallant knight, and pledged a lady
    word,
Thou wouldst have braved the billows blue all with thy naked
    sword ! "

22

"Oh, I will enter a cloister, and learn the monkish lore!
But know, thou haughty Liselil, thou'lt see my face no more!"

23

"Oh, go thy ways where'er thou wilt, let all thy prating be!
For had I bread and cheese for two, there should be none for
thee!"
—I will ride forth to seek for a fair one.

BIBLIOGRAPHY

CHILD, F. J. (ed.). The English and Scottish Popular Ballads.
5 volumes. 1882–98.

Selection from Child's collection, edited by H. C. SARGENT and
G. L. KITTREDGE. 1904.

GARBORG, HULDA. Norske Folkeviser.

GRUNDTVIG, S. (ed.). Danmarks Gamle Folkeviser. 5 volumes.
1853–1890. Translations into Danish of British Ballads.

GUMMERE, F. B. Article on *Ballads* in the *Cambridge History
of English Literature*. 1908.

HENDERSON, T. F. The Ballad in Literature. (*Cambridge
Manuals*.) 1912.

KER, W. P. Epic and Romance. 1897.

OLRIK, A. Danske Folkeviser i Udvalg, og Indledning. 1912.

PINEAU, L. Les Vieux Chants Populaires Scandinaves. 1898.

VIGFUSSON, G., and POWELL, F. YORK. Corpus Poeticum
Boreale. 2 volumes. 1883.

www.ingramcontent.com/pod-product-compliance
Ingram Content Group UK Ltd.
Pitfield, Milton Keynes, MK11 3LW, UK
UKHW042144280225
455719UK00001B/89